Finding Hope,
Healing, and Honor

Keepers
OF THE
faith

Five Native
Women Share
Their Stories

by Debra Fieguth

Sequoyah
EDITIONS

KEEPERS OF THE FAITH

Five Native Women Share Their Stories

by Debra Fieguth

A Sequoyah Edition

An imprint of Indian Life Books

A Division of Intertribal Christian Communications

ISBN 0-920379-20-6

First published November 2001

© 2001 Intertribal Christian Communications

Cover and interior design by Uttley/DouPonce DesignWorks, Sisters, Oregon, www.uddesignworks.com

Printed and bound in Canada.

Visit Indian Life Ministries' website at www.indianlife.org

*To Bessie, Helen, Lizzie,
Mavis, and Venus*

ACKNOWLEDGMENTS

When Indian Life Books phoned me one day and asked if I would be interested in writing a collection of profiles of native Christian women, it didn't take me long to say yes. Native culture, history and experience have always been close to my heart, and I knew there were many strong Christian women in the native community who had much to share—with their own people as well as with others.

When we sat down to discuss whom to include in the book, we looked for women who represented a range of tribal affiliations and geographical locations; women who demonstrated an uncompromising Christian faith in daily lives, ministry and secular work; women who would shine as a light among their own.

There are others out there besides these five—God has done great and wonderful things among his native daughters—but space and other factors made it impossible to include them all.

These are the stories of five brave women—brave because, despite tragedy, hardship and heartache, they were willing to talk about their lives so that others might be inspired and encouraged.

It wasn't always easy, for them or for me. More than once I was moved to tears as someone recounted a traumatic incident or recalled an abusive childhood or remembered a sorrow from the past. More than once I was angered by things that were wrong: systemic injustice, harsh treatment or unthinking prejudice. But many, many more times I was awed: by hope when despair might have seemed more natural; by faith despite overwhelming odds; by sheer determination and strength of spirit.

These are sacred stories, because God has moved, shaped, taught, delivered, forgiven and sustained each of these women with His great love, His compassion and His faithfulness.

Besides many hours of personal and telephone conversations, there were additional sources for some of the stories. One of the women, Helen Francis, wrote a book of her own, *Struggle to Survive*, from which most of her story in this book is taken. A book about the 1990 Oka crisis, *People of the Pines: The Warriors and the Legacy of Oka*, by Geoffrey York and Loreen Pindera (Boston: Little, Brown, 1991), provided background for the dramatic events of Mavis Etienne's life. Bessie McPeek's father, Leslie Garrett, recounted his experiences among the Ojibway of northwestern Ontario in *My Album of Memories*, published by Western Tract Mission in Saskatoon. Some of the information on Bessie's early life and that of her parents is taken from this book.

Thank you to Jim Uttley and the others at Indian Life Books who had the idea for this book and worked hard to bring it about. Thank you to my husband and friend, Ian Ritchie, whose heart is with mine in loving and wanting to learn from our native sisters and brothers, and who encouraged me and listened to me as I worked through the stories.

Thank you to Bessie, Helen, Lizzie, Mavis, and Venus for trusting me with your lives and your stories. Your courage and vulnerability, your faith and strength will speak to many. You inspire me to deeper faith, and I know you will inspire others.

—Debra Fieguth

FOREWORD

My earliest childhood memories include the love and laughter of my Metis [Cree and French] aunts. Though my father's family is very large, two women were particularly precious to me. Little did I know that God would bless me with their care in the final decades of their lives. The youngest (94!) passed away in the summer of 2001. With them in mind, I am especially honored to write this Foreword to Debra's important work.

Although my one aunt had spent years teaching school on remote reserves, loving the children as only a childless woman could, I learned early in life that the word "Indian" was to be whispered when applied to our family.

In private conversation, the aunts were proud of the resourcefulness and the strength of the Cree family women, including my grandmother. They told of her creative ability to sew beautiful garments and of the meals she prepared. They recounted the role their grandfather, Jean Baptiste Beauchemin, had played in Louis Riel's attempts to protect his people's land and lifestyle in Western Canada. Yet, societal pressures had taught them that it was safer to pass as "French"; it was best to distance themselves from the pain and loss of privilege that was a part of their Indian heritage.

When faced with similar pressures, not everyone can or will deny their heritage—though no one should be placed in a position of having to make that choice. The women Debra has profiled here, rather than denying who God created them to be, have embraced all they are and have allowed God to be present in their daily lives. They have sought peace instead of revenge; healing in place of bitterness; dignity not shame.

Debra has done well to bring the tales of these native women to a wider audience. Her stories are warm and honest. The women Indian Life Books has chosen reflect the strength and resourcefulness of the many native women I love and respect. Her readers will be encouraged by the real life triumphs—often in spite of incredible hardship—of real women. Native readers will know that these five stories represent a multitude of other women who have triumphed in difficult circumstances. Non-natives who have never had the opportunity to personally know native people, will be introduced to a new reality and will come away enriched.

Even though I know three of the women Debra writes about, I have learned new things about them as I have read these stories. A few times I tried to read the manuscript in public places, but set it aside as I wanted to let the tears flow freely. These women have made themselves so vulnerable. It is my prayer that they will be rewarded for their openness and honesty. There can be no greater reward than that lives are touched and changed for God's glory by these, their stories.

—WENDY PETERSON
Instructor, Providence College and Seminary
Otterburne, Manitoba

VENUS COTE

"I forgive You"

The pain was excruciating and it wouldn't go away. Venus Cote didn't even want to drink, which was what she spent most of her days doing. Sharp pains were ripping through her stomach. She had to get to a hospital.

Venus pulled on her coat and boots, left her grandmother's house on the Cote Reserve and headed for the road. It was a cold morning in January 1985 when she hitch-hiked into nearby Kamsack and found the hospital.

The emergency doctor quickly examined her and told her she would have to be admitted. Alcohol was poisoning her body. She was twenty-four years old.

Was this what she wanted? To die a slow, suicidal death from drinking too much?

※◎※◆◎◎◆◎◎※

Charlotte Cote, the daughter of Alice and Cecil Cote and the eldest of their nine children, gave birth to her first daughter, Venus, on July 23, 1960 at the Kamsack Union Hospital. The Saulteaux family lived on a small reservation bearing their family name, five miles northwest of Kamsack, located in eastern Saskatchewan near the Manitoba border. By the time Venus was born, her biological father was no longer a part of her mother's life, and her stepfather named her after a little girl he had read about in a story book. The couple had two daughters together, Donna and Beverly.

Venus doesn't remember her mother. She only knows what she was told about her.

One morning Cecil Cote, who customarily checked up on the family every day, went to Charlotte's place to see how she was doing. What he found there was a horror and a father's worst nightmare: his eldest daughter, Charlotte, was dead. She had been killed by her common-law husband. The three terrified little girls were huddled under the kitchen table.

Venus was only three years old. Her little sisters were just babies. Venus never told her grandparents what she had seen. But she had seen something, and it was enough to traumatize her into silence.

She was never the same after that. For a long time Venus would stand at her grandmother's window, looking out onto the road, tears rolling down her cheeks, wondering when her mother would be coming, knowing that she was never again going to come walking up that road.

It was heartbreaking for her grandparents, aunts and uncles to see. They were already angry and wounded over Charlotte's death. When the Cotes' eldest son committed suicide not long after that, the tragedy was too hard for them to bear, and they began drinking to cover up their pain.

But Alice and Cecil loved their little granddaughters, and willingly took them into their home and raised them. Though Alice knew English, she would only speak Saulteaux to the girls. "I love you," she would tell them in Saulteaux.

Venus grew up playing with her sisters, her cousins and her aunt Vera, who was only seven when the girls came to stay with their grandparents. Venus went to kindergarten on the reservation, then attended Victoria School in Kamsack.

School was a good time, maybe one of the best times of her young life, if only because it was a safe haven away from the atmosphere of constant drinking at home. White and native kids mixed together easily, not noticing differences in color or culture. Venus made friends with a white girl named Velvet, and the two used to eat their lunches together daily, swapping sandwiches when the other's lunch looked more interesting.

Academics didn't interest Venus, however. She did the

minimum amount of work, and it showed. She ended up repeating some grades.

Religion was never a big part of her life but Venus grew up believing in God, a God she wanted to have nothing to do with because if He was supposed to be in control of what was happening in life He wasn't doing a very good job. Her grandmother, raised a Roman Catholic, and her grandfather, who came from a United church, attended a local mission church but didn't make it a requirement for their children or grandchildren. Alice Cote, respected as an elder in the community, also sometimes took her small granddaughters to sundances on the reserve.

✖✦✖✦✖

When she was fourteen Venus had two friends who made a big impact on her life, but in entirely different ways.

One of them was Claudette, a native girl who started going to a Pentecostal church, wearing skirts instead of slacks and singing gospel duets with her sister. Claudette would sometimes talk to Venus about what she believed.

"God loves you," she told Venus one day. "Jesus loves you and He died for you."

Venus had never heard those words before and couldn't believe them. "I didn't believe that a God could love me and yet inflict so much hurt on one family and one person," she says. It was because of God that she was motherless, she told Claudette. It was because of God that she was fatherless. Her biological father, whom she had only known by name, had died; her stepfather, who had killed her mother, was in jail; and her grandfather, who had raised her, had also died. "It just seemed like I was an orphan and nobody loved me."

So Venus rejected what Claudette told her about God's love. So many in her extended family were drinking, and her future didn't look bright at all. So if anyone ever mentioned God, she didn't want to hear anything more about it.

Instead she chose to follow the influence of another friend.

One day this friend invited her to have a drink of booze she had stolen from her grandfather. So at fourteen, Venus took her first drink. Since the two spent a lot of time together, drinking became a habit. "When I hung out with her, I knew that's what we'd be doing."

It wasn't that she exactly liked drinking, but she discovered it to be a solution of sorts. "I never drank to enjoy it," she recalls. "I drank to forget a lot of things. It was sort of a remedy for not having to think, and for covering a lot of emotions. That's when I realized it was the answer to all my problems."

At least she thought it was. By the time she was seventeen she was still in Grade eight at Kamsack Junior High. She couldn't keep up with going to school and pursuing her career as an alcoholic. She had to choose, and she chose booze.

Free from school, Venus took off for Calgary, Alberta, several hundred miles west, with some friends and babysat their kids while they worked during the week. On weekends all of them would party. "Party" is a relative term, though. If a party is an occasion where everyone is happy and celebrating, this was something else. This was just sitting in a room and drinking beer after beer after beer.

"I wasn't happy," Venus admits. "For as long as I can remember, I never really was happy."

In fact, she was deeply unhappy, and drinking was the only way she knew of to dull the pain of loneliness and anger. She always wore dark colors, never anything lighter than black or navy. The darkness matched the feelings inside her, feelings she so desperately tried to suppress. She felt she had nothing worth living for, even though she knew her family cared for her.

During those years as a teenager and a young woman she thought of suicide often. If only she could just kill herself and end all her misery. But she was so insecure she was afraid to try, thinking she would probably not do it right and end up disabled and as miserable as ever. "I think that's what stopped me," she says now.

Instead she took the slow route. If she drank enough, she reasoned, she would die anyway, and what would it matter?

❖❖❖◆❖❖◆❖❖

Venus was back in Kamsack after living in Calgary for a few years. Her family realized alcohol had taken over her life, and begged her to stop, telling her she would kill herself if she didn't. One day her young aunt, Vera, who was also drinking, announced she was going to enter a treatment program.

"Why don't you come with me?" she asked her niece. She said she didn't want to go alone, but she probably had a secret motive—to get her niece, who had a worse drinking problem than she did, into treatment. So Venus, who was close to her aunt, went along and entered the twenty-eight-day program at New Dawn treatment center in the Qu'Appelle Valley.

It was the first time in a very long time that she was sober. At New Dawn, without the mask of alcohol, she realized there was somebody special hiding behind the dark colors and the sad exterior. There was a person who was capable of caring for others, and a person who had the potential to be happy. For the first time in years, Venus smiled. Others noticed her smile and commented on how beautiful it was.

For Venus, New Dawn was a new beginning. With the help of Alcoholics Anonymous meetings, she managed to stay sober for a few years.

✵◈✦◈✵✦◈✵◈✵

After going through the New Dawn program, Venus got a job at the treatment center for a while. Then she worked for the summer in the kitchen at a resort in the Qu'Appelle Valley. Later she applied for a job at a treatment center in Ile-a-la-Crosse, a small, mostly native community in a diagonally opposite area of Saskatchewan, the northwest. She was working there when she met a guy who told her he cared for her and wanted to take her away to British Columbia, two provinces west, to live.

She gave up everything for him. She quit her job and moved further south to Meadow Lake. But when she got there, he phoned her up and said "we're finished."

"I was furious," Venus remembers. "I was angry and I was hurt. And the first thing I thought of doing was drinking. So I started drinking again."

But this time she decided she needed to do something else besides drink, so she also started taking classes to upgrade her high school education. At school she met another young woman, Sarah, and the two became close friends. They spent a lot of time together, going to classes, drinking and talking.

Sarah described herself as a backslidden Christian. She believed in Jesus but wasn't living for Him anymore. When the two weren't drinking, Sarah would tell Venus about how she used to sing in church, and what her life was like when she was walking with the Lord. Venus grew to trust and respect Sarah very much.

"Where do people go who don't believe in Jesus Christ?" Venus asked her friend one day.

Sarah answered very carefully. "They don't enter the Kingdom of Heaven," she told Venus. "They wander around in darkness."

Sarah believed but she struggled. She ended up in a destructive way of life, drinking booze and living with a man who was cruel to her.

Venus left Meadow Lake and went back to Calgary, where she worked a bit at a bottle depot and spent the rest of her time drinking. Somehow she always had a place to stay, and she always had enough money to get drunk.

Some days while recovering from a hangover, Venus would turn on the TV and watch Billy Graham at a crusade. Her mind was too unfocused to understand what he was saying, but what she really liked was listening to George Beverly Shea singing hymns. She loved his deep voice, and listening to songs like "The Old Rugged Cross."

"It sort of made me wish that life was different," she recalls, "but not to the point where I wanted to change it. I thought a lot about things like that. I knew I drank a lot for a young person. I knew that life wouldn't last very long if I kept up the way I was going."

She ended up in a treatment center again, and it was there that she heard the news about her good friend Sarah. Sarah had died three months earlier. Her common-law husband had killed her and tried to make it look like a suicide. The news was devastating to Venus. If anyone had made an impact on her life, it had been Sarah.

Over the years Venus went into treatment programs several times. In Calgary, she roomed with a sixteen-year-old girl named Susie. Susie had also had a difficult life, but when she was sober she had found something else to fulfil her needs. For hours she would sit on her bed reading the Bible. She never preached to Venus about what she read, but sometimes Venus would ask her questions, and Susie would tell her how she became a Christian. Susie regularly went with her friends to a coffeehouse named the Burning Bush, and from there the young people would go out on the street and hand out tracts.

Later Venus roomed with another girl named Sharon. Sharon wasn't a Christian but members of her family were. On Sundays they would pick Sharon up for church, and one time they invited Venus along. Sharon's cousin, a native evangelist named Ross Shingoose, was preaching. Venus doesn't remember what he said, only that at the end of the sermon he gave an invitation. "There are two people here who aren't Christians," he said, inviting them forward to accept Jesus into their lives.

"He's talking about us," Sharon whispered to Venus. "Let's go up there." The problem was that Sharon wasn't serious. She only wanted to respond so her cousin wouldn't bug her. So the two went forward, repeated a prayer and left. Venus never went back to the church, and her life continued the same unhappy way that it had been.

She started drinking again and was kicked out of the treatment center. She and Sharon lived together for a while, until one day they found themselves in a car with friends somewhere in Saskatchewan. Venus was so drunk she didn't even remember leaving Calgary.

The car was stopped by the police, who discovered that Sharon, who was on parole from the Kingston Penitentiary for Women, had violated her parole. She was sent back to jail. Venus went back to Kamsack, then back to Calgary, where she stayed for a while before she returned to Kamsack to live with her grandmother again. She didn't have a job, and spent most of her time drinking with her grandmother.

✶✧✦✧✦✧✦✧✦✧✦✧✦

Here she was, lying in the hospital bed and thinking about her life. She had nothing, and she had nowhere to go. She had nothing to show for her life.

She was at the bottom.

It was January 10, 1985. As she lay there contemplating her life, she began to think of all the people who had told her about Jesus. She remembered Claudette, her school friend who was the first person ever to tell her that God loved her. She thought of Susie, who quietly read the Bible and answered questions about her faith. She recalled her friend Sharon's family, who took her to church. She remembered seeing Billy Graham on TV and listening to Bev Shea sing about the Old Rugged Cross.

And she remembered her dear friend Sarah, who had taught her so much about believing in Jesus even though she struggled with her own life. Where was Sarah now? Had she entered the Kingdom of Heaven?

Maybe Jesus is the answer after all, Venus wondered. Maybe what people say about Him is true. Maybe He is who He says He is.

She was alone in the room. The only way she knew how to pray was to tell God she was willing to give Him a chance.

"I'm willing to believe," she said aloud. Only God could hear her.

✖✦✖✦✖✦✖

Her words were few and softly spoken, but something changed. For one thing, when she got out of the hospital, she never drank again. For another, Jesus came into her life like she had been told He would. And He did love her. He really loved her.

For the first time ever in her life, she was happy. Jesus was taking away all the pain, the anger, the bitterness, even the bad memories. She read in the Bible that if she cast her burdens and cares on Jesus, He would take them from her.

It didn't mean life was suddenly easy, but now she had a means to get her through hard times. She lived with her grandmother for the next several months, and there was still drinking in the house. Sometimes when the others were drinking Venus would go outside, sit leaning against a wall and cry, calling out to God. "Where are you when I need you?"

"He was there all the time," Venus says now, "because He gave me what it took not to take the drink."

Venus wanted to tell some of her old friends about what had happened to her. She phoned up Sharon, her friend from the treatment center in Calgary. Venus reminded her about the time they went to church when Sharon's cousin was preaching, and about what her family believed about Jesus.

"I'm serving that same God," Venus told her. "I'm a born

again Christian." She told Sharon that she, too, had to get right with God.

Sharon wasn't moved. "That life might be for you but it's not for me," she told Venus. She didn't want to have anything more to do with Venus. A couple of years later Sharon died of cirrhosis of the liver.

Missionaries in the area, Frank and Mary Brown, and Jack and Brenda Cousins, held services on the reserve. Venus began attending church and taking part in Bible studies. A couple of her aunts and some of her cousins also became Christians, and in August, Venus and the others boarded an old orange school bus with the missionaries, and headed to nearby Madge Lake, where they were baptized.

⚝⚝⚝⚝⚝⚝

So what was she going to do with this new life? The missionaries suggested she go to Bible school, but she wasn't interested. Maybe it was too soon.

Then she met a gospel singer, Kene Jackson, who had graduated from Key Way Tin Bible Institute, located in Lac La Biche, Alberta, and geared for native students. Kene encouraged Venus to apply there.

She did, not thinking much of it. It was already summer, and she figured if she didn't hear back from the school by the end of summer she wasn't meant to go. She forgot about her application and stayed home.

Early the next January she received a call from the school. She was accepted, and she was supposed to be there within days. She still didn't want to go. She had nothing: no money, no decent clothes; she didn't even own a dress. The only useful thing she had was a Good News Bible.

Then Kene Jackson came to town again with his gospel band, Sonrise. "So, are you going to Key Way Tin?" he asked her.

"I didn't hear from them," she fibbed.

Kene was puzzled about why the school wouldn't let her know anything. He said he'd call Key Way Tin the next day and ask them what was going on.

Caught in her lie, Venus had to confess to him that yes, she had heard and she was accepted. "But I don't have any money to go," she protested.

"I'll give you fifty dollars to get you started," Kene said. Venus laughed inside. Fifty dollars wouldn't go very far.

Kene made her promise to go home and pray about whether to go to Bible school. So that night, Venus got down on her knees and prayed, "Lord, I'm willing to go to Bible school. But I don't have anything," she reminded God.

The next day she went to visit her missionary friends, Jack and Brenda Cousins, at the used clothing store they ran. Jack was just getting off the phone when she walked in the door.

There was good news: A church in Winnipeg had offered to pay for her first month room and board at Bible school, as well as tuition for the year! The generosity moved her. Perhaps she was meant to go after all.

Next, Brenda went through her closet and came up with a wardrobe for Venus. The two just happened to be the same size in everything, from dresses to shoes. Brenda outfitted her with the clothes she needed to be a student. Suddenly she had nicer clothes than she'd ever had before.

"But I don't have a bus ticket," she ventured, still testing the waters. Lac La Biche was many hours away, in northern Alberta, and a ticket would be expensive.

No matter. Kene and Jack had been scheming to get her to school, and came up with the money for the ticket.

So off she went on the bus, in early January 1986, barely a year after she had accepted Jesus into her heart, wondering what was happening in her life. She had no idea what she was getting into.

Venus spent the next three and a half years studying the Bible and learning about ministry. The experience gave her lots of time to think about what she wanted to do with her life.

✦✦✦✦✦✦

Before Venus became a Christian her life was characterized by anger. She was especially angry at her stepfather, whose actions had torn apart her life. And now, as a young believer, she was hearing from other Christians that she had to forgive.

She wasn't quite ready, or willing. "When God tells me to forgive, I'll forgive," she told people.

During her first year in Bible school she came across Jesus' words in Matthew that spoke to her: "For if you forgive men for their transgressions, your heavenly Father will also forgive you. But if you do not forgive men, then your Father will not forgive your transgressions" (Matthew 6:14, 15).

She realized that God had forgiven her sins, and yet she wasn't willing to forgive someone else. She knew she had to forgive her stepfather.

But how could she do that on her own? Venus had to ask God to help her. She began to pray that she would love her stepfather. Within herself, she knew, she didn't have what it took; she didn't love the man. She had spent her life plotting against him and harboring vindictive feelings towards him. She got others to beat him up on her behalf. If she saw him on the street, she would cross to the other side. If she did speak to him, the words would be hateful. She wanted him dead, or at least hurt, the way he had hurt her.

Now she asked God to give her compassion for her stepfather—the same kind of compassion that Christ had for her.

God answered her prayers. She was filled with love, compassion, and a spirit of forgiveness for the man who had killed her mother and ruined her childhood.

There was only one thing left to do: tell him.

✦◈✦◈✦◈✦

Venus had no idea where her stepfather was. She only knew he was in jail somewhere. So she began to pray that she would be able to locate him. Not long after that she received a letter in the mail from someone who had the address of the jail where he was incarcerated.

Asking God to give her the courage and the words to say, Venus got out some paper and a pen and began to write. She told her stepfather of her conversion, how Jesus had changed her life. She told him she needed to make things right with him.

"I need to ask your forgiveness for the way I've treated you," she wrote. She was filled with remorse for all the times she had spoken cruelly to him and plotted against him.

"I have forgiven you for what you have done," she continued. "What Jesus has done for me, He can do for you."

"I love you," her letter concluded. Her words were sincere, but she was only able to write them with God's help.

Not long afterwards, she got a reply from her stepfather. He told her that he had forgiven her for what she had done and thought against him. He told her that he loved her as his own child. He was, after all, the father of her two sisters, and the only father she had ever known as a small child. In his eyes, she had always been his little girl.

⬦⬦⬦⬦⬦⬦⬦

In 1990, Venus's grandmother, Alice Cote, died, and Venus went back to Kamsack for the funeral. In the meantime, God had been speaking to her about talking to her stepfather face to face. He had finished serving his sentence and was back in Kamsack.

There she saw him, sitting in a car. She approached the car and asked him if he would like to go for coffee. He agreed.

Over coffee, she told him that when she was a little girl she had seen what he had done to her mother. She told him again that she had forgiven him and that she loved him, and she promised she would never use that information to speak against him.

He sat there with tears rolling down his face. "I always wondered what you saw," he said.

In 1998 he had a heart attack. Venus happened to be in Kamsack at the time, so she went to visit her stepfather in the hospital.

"You've done some terrible things in your life," she told him. "But God is able to forgive that. You don't have to live with that guilt. You don't have to live with that on your conscience."

"I love you," Venus told him again. "But God loves you much more than I can ever love you."

The next day she went to see him again. She shared the gospel message with him, that Jesus had died for his sins and could forgive him. She told him she wanted to share heaven with him someday.

Although he never spoke words of remorse for killing her mother, Venus sensed it in him. "He was forgiven," she explains. "I didn't need to hear it anymore. I saw it on his face."

Venus's stepfather died several months later. Looking back, her desire is that he be remembered, not as a murderer, but as a person who had good qualities; a person who was capable of change, and who did change.

"I always used to say that I never had a father," Venus reflects. Now she believes that's not true. "There was no doubt that he loved me when he was there," she says. "He was the only father that I had and that I knew."

❖❖❖✦❖❖❖✦❖❖❖

In the summer after her first year at Bible school, Venus went back to Kamsack to work and help her grandmother. The second summer, 1987, she took the Northern Missionary Training Camp run by Northern Canada Evangelical Mission.

"I wasn't going to be a missionary," she recalls. She only took the internship program because several of her girlfriends from school had applied. "We were going to have all kinds of fun if we were put on the same reserve."

But the mission decided Venus Cote, who was now twenty-seven years old, was a mature student and could be sent all the way to New Brunswick to work with a missionary there. "They had no idea what they were getting," she laughs.

That summer, at the Eel River Bar Reserve near Dalhousie, changed her life. She realized how challenging and difficult it was to be a missionary. For six weeks she lived on the reservation.

One day she and her partner Joanne Plett went to visit an elderly woman on the reservation. They told her what they were doing, that they were sharing about Jesus with the people in the community.

"I'm Catholic!" the woman retorted. "No one is going to

change my religion, and I'm going to die Catholic." That made Venus think about what she was doing and how she was misunderstood. She wasn't trying to change anybody's religion. She only wanted to talk to them about the Bible, and about Jesus.

The Mi'kmaq people were friendly but they weren't interested in the gospel. They were curious about the newcomer, but that was it. Kids would come over to visit Venus and Joanne and play, but they didn't want to hear Bible stories.

Nevertheless, Venus went back to Bible school excited about her summer and announced that she was ready to be a missionary.

⬥✦✦✦⬥

During her first couple of years at KBS, Venus had become interested in South America. She grew to love the natives of South America, and looked forward to working with them some day. She talked constantly about going to live with the Spanish-speaking people in South America.

What she didn't want was to be a missionary to native people in North America. She knew from her own experience and past negative attitude to the gospel that her people would be difficult to work with, that they might reject her. She didn't want to be rejected. "I didn't want any hardship," she says, "I guess because I had given missionaries a hard time." Even as a young Christian Venus had antagonized the local missionaries, Mary and Frank Brown. One day when Mary came to visit her Venus told her she didn't want to be a Christian anymore because it was too hard.

"I chased her out of the house. She gave me a few days and came back."

That summer after Bible school, 1988, she was invited to go on tour with the school's summer ministry team, the Torchbearers. The team traveled throughout British Columbia, Alberta and Saskatchewan, giving their testimonies, singing and holding services. In Alberta they led a children's camp near Hobbema.

At the end of camp her heart was broken. It was time for the children to go home and they didn't want to go. They clung to the back of the bus that was to take them home, refusing to get on and crying. "You love us here," they said. "Can't we stay?"

Venus knew these children needed to know and understand God's love. And who was to share God's love with them?

She went down to the dock at the lake and sat there. It was raining, and the rain mingled with the tears running down her cheeks. "All right, Lord," she prayed. "If you want me to be a missionary to my own, I'm willing."

She asked God to replace her love for South America with a love for her own people, and He answered her prayer.

Venus Cote graduated from Key Way Tin Bible Institute in the spring of 1989 and went straight into the Missionary Development Program operated by a coalition of agencies working with natives in Canada. In the meantime she had applied to Northern Canada Evangelical Mission.

The questionnaire asked her where she would prefer to be placed. She believed she wanted to stay in central Canada among people she was familiar with. But when it came to the interview, she learned that she had written "eastern Canada" on the application instead! The organization told her she was being sent to the Maritimes.

Venus didn't argue. She accepted the decision as God's will, and in January 1990 she moved to Campbellton, New Brunswick to work with the Mi'kmaq.

A lot had happened in the five short years since she had become a Christian. Once antagonistic towards God, here she was about to spend the rest of her life telling people about Him.

<hr/>

Being a village missionary had its challenges. People were often suspicious that this newcomer was trying to change their religion. Many of the older people were devout Catholics. Many of the younger ones were not religious at all—until they found out Venus was there to tell them about what the Bible says. Then, suddenly, they would identify themselves as Catholics, and therefore not in need of someone to talk about religion with them.

Her advantage was that she was native. They were curious about this woman from a different tribe and different place who had come so far away from home to live among them. Being native opened doors for Venus. The people wanted to know more about her. And despite differences between the Mi'kmaq and Saulteaux cultures, there was a common value: natives take care of their own. Because she was so far away from home, the people kept their eye on Venus, befriending her and helping her.

The early years of mission work focused on visiting people rather than trying to do something too structured. Because Venus grew up on a reservation, she had an understanding of what reservation life was like, how people thought and how they did things. There were differences: out west, people tend to hang out in the shopping malls; in the Maritimes, if she wanted to go where the people were, it wasn't the malls; they tended to stay home on the reservation. If they were drinking, it wouldn't usually be in public, but in the privacy of their homes.

She could empathize with those who had problems with alcohol. Remembering her own painful childhood, she became burdened for children growing up in an atmosphere where alcohol dominated. Her main desire was to offer them hope: life didn't have to be an endless generational cycle of alcohol abuse. Things could change, and the whole pattern of family life could be different.

But the highlight of every year was summer camp. That was when all the local children would come together for water activities and listening to Bible stories. That was when relationships with children had a chance to grow stronger.

The young missionary moved around to different parts of New Brunswick and Nova Scotia, working first in Campbellton,

New Brunswick and then moving to Sydney, on Nova Scotia's Cape Breton Island, and back to New Brunswick, this time settling in Belle Isle Creek.

After camp would come follow-up visiting. It was difficult work for Venus because she had to spend a lot of time traveling by herself, moving from one community to another to visit the kids who had been to camp that summer. In village work you see the same people all the time, she points out. In camp work, a few months might go by before you see people again. "It was a lonely job," she reflects.

She moved to Shubenacadie, Nova Scotia, in the mid-1990s so she could be closer to her field directors as well as a co-worker with whom she could have fellowship. Then she moved to Truro, where she was going to church.

In 1998 she was called to Fredericton, the capital of New Brunswick, to work with a different tribe, the Maliseet. The people are related to the Mi'kmaq, but different, the way Cree and Saulteax are related but different. For one thing, while the Mi'kmaq are friendly and outgoing, the Maliseet are more reserved. They don't welcome newcomers with open arms, Venus found.

Whether they are from the reservations or from urban centers, summer camp is the place where children come to be loved. Often lacking in attention at home, they eagerly latch onto camp staff, sitting on their laps and basking in loving hugs. "All they need is for you just to love them, just as they are," says Venus.

Parents have mixed motives for sending their children to camp. Since the local band offices usually pay the campers' fees, sometimes adults take advantage of the offer just so they can have a vacation from looking after their kids. They don't usually send them so the children can hear the gospel. In fact, sometimes they tell their kids they can go to camp as long as they don't listen to the Bible stories!

Though the camp offers crafts, canoeing, archery and other activities, more than anything the kids enjoy swimming and playing in the water. Because the camp is small—they don't take more than fifty kids a week—they get lots of the individual attention they crave.

During the school year, ministry to children sometimes takes the form of after-school clubs. But clubs can only be held if the band office provides space, or if a local family is able and willing to host.

The work is slow and hard, like pioneer missionary work, and often discouraging. "You think you're getting somewhere, and things are looking good and people are listening, and then people you thought were doing well aren't doing well. It's really hard," Venus reflects. "We tell ourselves that we have to be faithful. Because if we have to rely on what happens we'd always be discouraged."

Sometimes, she admits, she feels like giving up. But if she left, who would replace her? "Who would love these people the same way I do? Who would care enough? Who would leave all their earthly possessions and their families?"

One year Venus made friends with a woman named Bonnie, who came to camp from Maine when she heard it was an "Indian camp" and that she would learn how to do native dances and make native crafts. The Bible camp turned out not to be what she expected. Nevertheless, Venus led her to the Lord that week, and followed up by traveling regularly to Maine to visit her.

Bonnie struggled. She wasn't sure where she fit. She was native, and wanted to take part in native culture. It seemed like she had to make a choice. One day she phoned Venus and told her she wasn't ready to live for Jesus, and that if she changed her mind she would let Venus know.

"She felt it was too much to give up," says Venus. Still, she believes that Bonnie was saved by Jesus. Maybe one day she will remember the love shown to her by Venus and turn back to Jesus, the way Venus remembered all those who had told her about Jesus that day in the hospital in 1985.

Many native people struggle over what is acceptable from their culture after they have given their lives to Jesus. There's a richness in culture, language and heritage that shouldn't have to be denied, Venus believes. But she is careful to encourage worship and practices that honor Jesus. If people deny Christ in their practices or worship, then it is wrong.

<hr />

Since moving to Fredericton, Venus has found a small United Baptist church to attend in nearby New Maryland, just outside the city. She went all over town looking for the right church to attend, and when she walked into the New Maryland church, she knew that was where she was supposed to be. The people have welcomed her and looked after her. They have respected the fact that she is a missionary and needs rest and nurture from her congregation.

And sometimes they have surprised her with special gifts. Before Christmas of 1999, someone asked her to meet at the local shopping mall. When she arrived, there were two women from the church with gift-wrapped packages to present to her. They had gone shopping and bought her a new wardrobe! It was evidence: God always provides for her needs, and even goes beyond what she asks for.

Venus has learned that she can ask God for something specific, and He answers. Though she lives on a small salary, sometimes she receives small luxuries that many other people would take for granted.

"People laugh at me because I pray for the littlest things," she says. For example, she had a small collection of CDs—but no stereo to play them on. She told people she was praying for a stereo. One day an aunt called her.

"Do you have any CDs?" she asked her niece.

"I have a few," Venus replied.

"Do you have a CD player?" her aunt asked.

"No," Venus replied.

"Why do you have CDs without a CD player?"

"I'm praying for one," Venus replied.

It turned out her aunt had a CD player to give her.

Little things like that, having faith in God to supply her needs but without being materialistic, speak to her non-Christian friends. They see how God has answered her prayers.

Venus wanted to go to Alberta in the summer of 2000 to visit some family members. She went to a travel agent and found out the cost of a flight to Edmonton was $800. Venus told the agent she didn't have that much money, but was able to pay the $50 deposit.

"She looked at me strange, like she shouldn't be booking this thing."

But several days later, Venus returned to the travel agent to pay the reminder of the ticket. She had $775, more than she needed to pay the balance.

The agent said to her: "I wasn't sure you were going to have the money."

It was another example of how her faith speaks to people.

New Year 2000. Venus was in Winnipeg visiting a friend when she got a call. Her sister Donna had overdosed, apparently accidentally, and was on life support in the hospital in Regina.

Venus quickly changed her plans and delayed her return to New Brunswick. When she got to Regina, she was told Donna had suffered brain damage but the doctors didn't yet know how much.

The doctors told Venus and other family members that

they could choose right then to take Donna off life support, or they could request a battery of tests to make sure there was no brain activity. After that, they would have seventy-two hours to decide.

The family requested the tests. The result—no brain activity. The choice was straightforward but difficult: Donna would be taken off life support. Venus remained at her sister's side as the life ebbed out of her.

"I think that was the hardest thing I ever had to do, was to see my sister die in front of me." Donna, one of the little sisters Venus had huddled with under the table the night their mother had died, was thirty-seven, with four children of her own. She, too, had suffered in her life, through choices she made, through a relationship that cost her. Now she was gone, and her sister had to learn, slowly, to accept her death.

❊❖✦❖❊✦❖❊❖

In mid-July of the same year, Venus was at camp in New Brunswick when she got another phone call, this one from an aunt. Her nineteen-year-old niece, Beverly's daughter, had died in a car accident.

Venus was angry and heartbroken. She went down to the lake and sat on a chair, weeping. "You've done it again!" she cried out to God. How could she possibly be expected to take another blow?

Another missionary came and sat down quietly beside Venus. "I don't want to hear anything Christian right now!"

Venus told her. Her co-worker didn't try to give her any advice, or talk her out of what she was feeling. She just quietly listened to her friend, while Venus lashed out in pain. "She got the brunt of the emotions that I was feeling," Venus said later. Venus also knew she couldn't feel anger forever. She apologized to her co-worker, and to God, as she began the difficult process, once again, of accepting a loss.

Later that summer Venus visited her sister in Edmonton, and after a vacation, returned to New Brunswick. One Sunday shortly afterwards she was speaking in a church when the realization came to her: yes, bad things do happen, but lots of good things happen too. The important thing was not to focus on all the sorrow that had happened in her life, but to realize God's faithfulness over the years.

"It always boils down to God's faithfulness and His promises and commitment," she reflects. "If I remain committed in my walk with Him it's not always going to be like this. In spite of all the heartaches I've had, even in this past year, I'm still able to smile knowing that He's still so much in control.

"Many times I didn't think I would make it, but He always gave me what I needed and He always sends someone my way. I always tell people not to feel sorry for me. It all boils down to what Christ has done. I couldn't have done it without Him. He's carried me through and He will do it again."

MAVIS ETIENNE

Proud to be a Mohawk

"Rycki!" Mavis Etienne shouted to her twenty-four-year-old son standing next to her car. "Rycki! Relax! They're trying to intimidate you!"

It was the summer of 1990, the height of the "Oka Crisis" when Mohawks squared off against the Canadian Army and the dreaded Sûreté du Quebéc (SQ), and the air was thick with tension.

The police were making arrests at random. That day Mavis, attempting to pass a roadblock to fetch gas and milk—desperately needed behind the barriers—was stopped by the army and then the police. When they ordered both her and her son out of the car, she knew what was coming next. Police customarily tried to harass and intimidate young men, forcing them to fight back so the SQ could then claim the young men resisted arrest. That's when she began yelling at her only son, Rycki. She didn't want him to fall for their tactics.

"Your son is under arrest," the police informed Mavis. The bewildered young man, heeding his mother, didn't try to fight back. As it turned out, attacking Rycki was only a ploy. The person they really wanted was his mother.

"Mrs. Etienne," the officer said, "you're under arrest."

But for what reason? Mavis, a counselor at Onen'to:kon Treatment Services, the Mohawk-run center for treating substance abuse, was one of the negotiators trying to bring about a peaceful settlement between the Mohawks, who did not want their land bulldozed to expand a golf course, and the government forces.

Police told her they were arresting her for intimidation and for being at the barricade constructed by the Mohawk people to protect their territory. And they had the pictures to prove it.

At that moment some film-makers from the National Film Board went by. "They're arresting me!" Mavis called to them so they could let people know at the treatment center that she was being arrested. The incident was filmed and later used in an NFB documentary, *Kanehsatake: 270 Years of Resistance.*

The whole thing was so bizarre. Police had let her husband, James, through the roadblock with no trouble, likely because his hair was red instead of black; he wasn't visibly Mohawk.

They put Mavis in an unmarked car, while Rycki followed in his mom's car.

For Mavis, the incident was one of the most dramatic in the seventy-eight-day standoff that resulted in the death of one SQ officer and no resolution to the dispute. Unwilling to be intimidated by the police, she firmly stood her ground when they harassed her. "I wasn't afraid," she says, "because I knew they were in the wrong, and I knew God was with me."

✦✦✦✦✦✦✦✦

Mavis Cree was born on November 20, 1944, the youngest of nine children, after Helen, Stanley, Sidney, Roger, Hubert, Wallace, Hilda and Noreen. She never knew her brother Hubert, who drowned in the lake a few months before Mavis was born, when he was nine years old.

How did a Mohawk family end up with the surname of Cree? "My great-great-grandfather came from Manitoba," Mavis explains. He was a Cree, but he married a Mohawk.

While her older siblings were all born at home, Mavis was born at the Royal Victoria Hospital in Montreal.

"You're going to have to choose which one will survive," the doctor informed her father, Morris Cree, when her mother, Susan, was pregnant with Mavis. Susan had a rare blood type, O Negative, and at forty years of age, was experiencing a very difficult pregnancy. The doctor didn't think she would survive if she carried the pregnancy to term.

But Morris Cree was unwilling to make that choice. "Save both of them," he said to the doctor. Miraculously, both survived, and both were healthy.

For the first two years of her life, the family lived in Kanehsatake, a Mohawk community forty-five miles northwest of Montreal. Though it covered a radius of only five miles, the territory was spacious. When she was two, the Cree family moved to Kahnawake, a smaller Mohawk territory located south of Montreal.

Childhood was happy. Kids rode their bikes around the community, where the houses were close together and everything was familiar. They could speak only Mohawk until they went to school and were forced to use English, and even then, they would secretly speak their mother tongue on the playground when the teacher wasn't listening.

On Sundays the family would have a traditional breakfast of cornbread, with white corn and kidney beans, and steak and gravy. Mohawk women had been corn growers for many years, sustaining the family economy with their crops. In the Mohawks' matrilineal society, Mavis was born into the Wolf clan; others were Turtles or Bears.

Mavis loved to climb trees, ride her bicycle and box. Her dad had a pair of boxing gloves which he gave to his sons, but little Mavis decided she wanted to use them. One time she was sparring with her cousin, who was two years younger, and though she was small for her age, she knocked him over. "I didn't know how strong I was!"

She was also an industrious little girl. When tourist buses came to the community, Mavis would go down to the Roman Catholic church where they parked and sell crafts made by some of the adults—little velvet birds decorated with beads, and beaded picture frames. The entrepreneurial skills she developed early in life, as well as her love of arts and crafts, became useful to her later as an adult.

She wasn't a perfect child. Like other kids, she pushed the boundaries, experimenting with how much she could get away with. As it turned out, in the Cree household, it wasn't much: when she and her friends stole a cigar and smoked it in the bathroom, Mavis got sick, her mom found out and she got a spanking; when she tried to steal a harmonica from a store, she dropped it and was caught; when she tried swearing, her mom washed her mouth out with soap.

Mavis's parents, though not well educated, did their best to raise their family well. Mavis's dad worked for a steel company and later a hydro company, while her mom cleaned houses in Montreal.

Her parents were good role models, teaching their children to be generous and helpful to others. "They had the gift of hospitality," Mavis recalls. "If there was a minister or missionary in town they would stay at our house and my mother would put on a spread." Most of the Cree children grew up to be in helping professions; three became pastors.

From the time she was very young Mavis learned about the Christian faith. Both her parents had become Christians before she was born, when Italian Pentecostal missionaries came to the area. Before the Pentecostals, there was a Methodist presence in the community. French Catholics had been in the area since the seventeenth century.

There was no doubt about the effect of faith on life. Mavis saw miracles with her own eyes. One time her mother was doubled up with pain from appendicitis. The church people prayed for her and she stood right up as if nothing was wrong!

Mavis made her own decision to accept Jesus as her Savior when she was eleven, just before the family moved from Kahnawake to Medina, New York. There was an evangelistic meeting at a big Pentecostal church in Montreal, and a man named Richard Vineyard was preaching. When he asked if anyone wanted to repent and follow Jesus, Mavis stood up and went forward.

"It made me realize I couldn't hang on what my parents were doing," she recalls. "I had to have my own relationship with God."

When the family moved to New York they joined a church that had lots of activities for young people, including Bible quizzes and youth conventions. Being part of the church helped Mavis to grow in her faith.

Mavis didn't mind that she wasn't allowed to do things other girls did, like go to dances or wear make-up. "I loved Jesus so much. I loved His Word."

Traditionally, Mohawks were known as "Kanienkehaka," or "people of the flint," which is the name many still prefer. They were named Mohawks, or "eaters of men," by the Algonquins, who were impressed with their warrior-like character.

From early on in life, Mavis was proud to be a Mohawk. Her parents were proud to be Mohawks, and taught their children to appreciate who they were. Because of the strong community the family lived in, Mavis was unaware of racism. "I didn't really think I was different as a child."

Her first clue that her people were not like other people came when they crossed the border into the U.S. The customs officers asked her parents their nationality. Instead of saying "Canadian," they always replied "Mohawk."

"Then I knew that we were different," says Mavis.

"People always wanted us to become citizens of one nation or another but we never would," she comments. There were Mohawks in Ontario, Quebec and New York, and the borders meant nothing to them. As a Mohawk nation, they believed they had the right to cross the border that had been artificially created. Fortunately, the Customs officials agreed, and let them travel back and forth as Mohawks rather than as Canadians.

Now, instead of holding a Canadian passport, Mavis carries a Mohawk passport.

After two years in Medina, where Mavis completed her junior high school, the Cree family moved to a nearby town, Middleport. When she was sixteen, her parents moved back to Canada, but Mavis stayed and finished her grade twelve in New York.

Following graduation, she went to Graham's Business College in Montreal, and then got a job in Manhattan with the American Foundation for the Blind.

Then she decided she wanted to study the Bible more, so she went to All Tribes Bible School in Phoenix, Arizona in 1963. She only stayed a year. Having had lots of Bible teaching already, "I found it too easy," she says. "To me it was like Sunday school." That's not to put down the Bible school; it's just that it was geared toward people who didn't already have much background in the Bible.

So she returned to her home community of Kanehsatake, where she was born, and there she has stayed ever since—except for numerous trips speaking and consulting across Canada and the U.S.

Before she went to Bible school, Mavis had begun dating a Finnish fellow who lived in Montreal. "You realize," she informed him when she left, "that when I come back this relationship is probably going to be over."

"I'll take that chance," he said. When she came back, renewed in her faith, she knew she could no longer go out with this young man, who wasn't a Christian. But he still wanted to see her. He suggested meeting in Montreal, where he was working. "Be on that bus at 6:30," he told her.

"What do you mean, 'be on that bus'?" she asked him. "Don't say 'be on that bus', say 'try to be on that bus'."

"Be on that bus," he repeated. Mavis didn't go, and the relationship ended.

Mavis was in church one day when her sister Noreen pointed out a redheaded fellow and commented, "he's kind of cute." Meanwhile, James Etienne's mother had been plotting. "The Cree sisters are back for the summer and they're going to be in church," she told her son.

So James went to church that evening, and that's where he met Mavis. They started dating soon afterwards. The two were married on July 17, 1965. Mavis's brother Roger performed the wedding ceremony in English and Mohawk, and her mother did all the cooking for the celebration meal at the community hall.

A year later their only child, Rycki, was born. While James worked outside in landscaping and yard work, Mavis stayed home to care for her son. She also picked up her earlier entrepreneurial skills and earned extra income by doing everything from selling Tupperware and encyclopedias (in order to get a free set for her son) to launching an arts and crafts cooperative.

She took an arts and crafts class in Kanehsatake, where she "caught the bug of doing beadwork." She beaded everything from moccasins to earrings, belts, book covers, wallets and hair ties. She even beaded her own deerskin dress. "I became a beadwork machine," she laughs. "I loved creating new things."

There were other crafts as well: pottery, weaving, and netting the pouches for lacrosse sticks, an important skill since the game of lacrosse originated with the Mohawk people. Crafts had always been a part of Mohawk culture; Mavis's maternal grandmother was a basket weaver. Some of Mavis's work has gone as far afield as Germany and Australia.

With a friend, Mavis started an arts and crafts association, which grew to include fifty members. They took their work to powwows in Quebec and the eastern U.S., demonstrating the crafts and selling them. Mavis later became president of the Indian Craftsmen of Quebec, a corporation that sold the artists' work throughout Canada.

※◇◆◇※◆◇◆※

Mavis's mother Susan was a faithful Christian and devoted mother and grandmother. Just sixteen when she married twenty-six-year-old Morris Cree, she took responsibility for her large family, spending hours on her knees praying for each one of them. She loved God's Word, and would read it aloud to her husband in Mohawk. She also translated gospel songs into Mohawk, an ability she had learned from her own mother, who had translated about one hundred songs. Many of Susan's translations appear in a gospel song book, although she was never given credit for her efforts. When her daughter sees a song in a book, she writes in her mother's name as the translator. "I know because I typed it!" she explains.

Susan Cree had a heart condition, and her health was deteriorating. She knew her time on earth might be short, so she made a point of making amends with people with whom she had disagreed. One of her unmarried granddaughters, for example, was having a baby. To show that she accepted and loved her granddaughter, Susan went out to buy things for the baby and presented them to the young mother-to-be.

It was 1972. Susan wanted a new bed. She asked her youngest daughter to help her shop for one and move it to her house. Mavis was tired from working that day, but she agreed to help her mother. Susan slept in her brand new bed one night, and had a heart attack the next day, a Sunday, and was taken to the hospital. She was sixty-seven.

The following Friday morning, Mavis went to visit her mother in the hospital, about forty-five miles from home. Her mom looked great. When James suggested they visit her again that evening, Mavis declined, since she was tired and thought she might just wait till Saturday to go back.

The next day she was at her parents' house when her niece Judy phoned. "I went to visit Grandma in the hospital and she passed away," Judy told her Aunt Mavis.

"Who's your grandmother?" Mavis couldn't believe who she was talking about.

"Your mother," Judy replied.

Mavis refused to believe her mother had died until she saw her body. The news was like a load of bricks falling on her. "Nobody can explain to you how it feels like when you lose your mom," she points out. "Nobody can replace a mom." Singing at her mother's funeral with her two sisters a few days later was one of the hardest things she had to do.

Her grief was alleviated by a dream, which she believes God gave to her as a necessary part of closure. In her dream, her mom was standing on a porch. Mavis said to her, "Mom, you died. Why are you here?"

"No, they revived me," her mother told her in the dream. Then she stepped forward and gave her daughter a big hug. "When I woke up I said, 'was that a dream, or was that for real?' It was so real." The dream gave Mavis comfort in the days and weeks ahead as she had to learn to live without her mother.

❉❉❉❉❉❉❉❉❉

All her life Mavis has loved volunteer work. She worked on several boards in the community, including the board that started a treatment center for chemical dependencies, Onen'to:kon Treatment Services in Kanehsatake. ("Onen'to:kon" means "under the pines.") Eventually she got trained as a counselor herself, and in 1987 started working at the center, taking the night shift in the residential program. After two years she became an outreach counselor, and soon after that she began counseling inside the center.

Several years later she became head of the clinical staff, overseeing outreach and in-house counselors at the sixteen-bed facility.

Culture plays a big part in the six-week program, which is based on the Alcoholics Anonymous twelve-step model.

Besides one-on-one counseling, there are talking circles, healing circles and lectures. Each person has a customized program for drug and alcohol treatment.

There are also family programs, which family members are required to take before they can visit the individual going through treatment. "We try to help the family, so when the person gets out, they're more supportive," Mavis explains.

Funded by Health Canada and operated by Mohawks, the treatment center serves the three local Mohawk territories and greater Montreal, but it also receives clients from northern Quebec, including Crees from the James Bay area and Inuit from even farther north.

Treatment is divided into two parts. For the first three weeks, participants are in the "Pathfinders" group, and for the second segment they are in the "Pathwalkers" group. "Talking circle" refers to a form of group therapy. "Healing circle" is a non-confrontational setting employing the traditional way of passing the eagle feather when someone takes a turn to talk.

Most clients don't come to the center to get rid of their addictions. They come because their families have put ultimatums on them: if you don't deal with your addiction, a wife might say, I'm leaving. But by the time the six weeks are over, they have learned to face the real issues behind the addictions.

The center's first aim is to get rid of all their excuses for drinking and doing drugs—excuses that include things like numbing the pain of never having felt a parent's love or hearing the words "I love you."

"I tell them if you never hear those words, you still have to sober up," Mavis says. "You have to sober up to stop the cycle, so your kids won't end up here." Too many natives have raised themselves because their parents aren't involved, and when they have children of their own they have no parental role model to follow. The cycle can be blamed in part on the damage that was done during the residential school era, when students were robbed of their culture and language. Some were even scrubbed with SOS pads to make them look lighter-skinned.

Most of the residential schools were run by churches. "That's why so many people are turned off from church," Mavis points out. "A lot of people wonder, if there was a loving God, why did this happen to me? If they were yanked from their parents, they didn't get parented and nurtured. They only learned abuse."

Having no pride, language or culture, having lost their respect for elders, and suffering the scars of abuse, many residential school survivors started drinking and doing drugs to numb the pain. Then they married partners who had had the same experience and the cycle was perpetuated.

The second aim of treatment is to get them to love themselves, because if they love themselves, Mavis points out, they won't want to do harm to their bodies and psyches.

The treatment center is unique in that it is spiritually based, but traditional believers and Christians work harmoniously side by side. "We get along very well because we respect each other's belief system," Mavis says.

Mavis is very careful not to compromise her Christian faith. "There's a lot of power in native spirituality," she points out, "and it's the unknown that scares people." Some non-traditionalist people don't like the chanting and drumming from the Plains, she points out, for example, because they don't understand what the chanting is about.

Yet Mavis won't put down the practices or beliefs of others. "You will never draw people to Jesus if you put down their beliefs," she reasons.

All clients who come into the center are asked to use their spiritual beliefs as a means to help them recover from drug or alcohol addiction. Some clients don't believe in anything, or don't know what they believe. Some believe in a Creator or God, but they blame Him for their problems. In any case, the counselors ask them to begin to pray.

Then they are asked to be grateful instead of complaining about their lives. Complaining just makes them more depressed. "If they start praying, they might start to think there's somebody out there." The ones who find a "higher power" usually have better success in overcoming their drug problems and related issues.

In recent years Mavis has traveled throughout North America giving workshops on addictions and sexual abuse. So many people are in denial over sexual abuse, she says. "They think if we don't talk about it, it's not really happening.

"But then if you look at the statistics and ask why people are killing themselves and drowning in booze, that's why." Often people don't want to talk about the abuse because the perpetrator was a relative or someone else close to the family.

❈❈❈❈❈❈

In the mid-1980s Mavis launched into another volunteer project when people in the community wanted to start their own radio station. Having experience in setting up non-profit corporations, she volunteered to help get it going. Besides, she recalls, "I wanted to be part of it to make sure the gospel got on the air."

As it turned out, her work was not just behind the scenes as she had planned. Since there weren't many volunteers for deejays, Mavis ended up hosting a program herself. When CKHQ began broadcasting, her voice speaking Mohawk was the first one that went over the air.

At first her one-hour, Sunday afternoon program was half country and western, half gospel. She played tapes from southern gospel groups and other favorites. But she didn't feel right about playing country and western songs, so after a while she switched to an entirely-gospel format. There was no lack of material, even when the program went to two hours and later four hours each Sunday. There were tapes by native Christian singers, including Mavis and two of her sisters, who formed the Mohawk Gospel Trio, as well as music by Mahalia Jackson and other well-known singers.

❈❈❈❈❈❈

The history of conflict between the Mohawks and the white people in southern Quebec goes back centuries. The Sulpicians, a French order of Roman Catholic priests, first came to the area in the mid seventeenth century, establishing a mission in Montreal in 1663. They took over the Island of Montreal in 1676, displacing the Mohawks to smaller tracts of land, including Kanehsatake.

But the Sulpicians kept asking the French king for more land, ostensibly to establish a place where they could more successfully evangelize the Mohawks and provide them with a place to fish, hunt and farm. The system of ownership followed a medieval feudal system, whereby a seigneury, or tract of land, is set up for tenants to work the land owned by lords. The problem was, of course, that the Mohawks weren't tenants.

But without the Mohawks realizing, the Sulpicians took legal "ownership" of the land, and in 1721 the last Mohawks left the Island of Montreal and went to Kanehsatake, an area that was also called Lake of Two Mountains.

The Royal Proclamation of King George III in 1763, four years after General Wolfe defeated Montcalm on the Plains of Abraham, guaranteed that the Mohawk lands were to be protected. The Mohawks fashioned a traditional "wampum belt" to signify their agreement to settle at the Lake of Two Mountains. The beaded belt featured a cross in the middle with men on either side. A long white line of beads symbolized the limits of the Mohawk territory. At each end was a dog, placed there to guard the territory. The Mohawks presented the belt to the superintendent of Indian Affairs in 1787 as proof of their title to the land.

The belt was rejected by the government as worthless. Meanwhile, the Sulpicians believed they owned the land, and could tell the Mohawks where to live and what to do. Despite several government inquiries into the land issue over the next sixty years, a government ordinance in 1840 recognized the Sulpician title to the Lake of Two Mountains seigneury.

Deprived of their ancestral lands, the Mohawks had difficulty making a living. They were punished for chopping down trees, even for their own use as fuel or for building homes. They were arrested for using wood to make and sell lacrosse sticks, snowshoes or baskets to earn money.

Sose Onasakenrat, known as Joseph Swan in English, was a bright young seminary student at the Sulpician college in Montreal. One of his classmates was a Metis fellow named Louis Riel, who later led his own fight for sovereignty in Manitoba and Saskatchewan, where he was hanged for treason in 1885. In 1868, twenty-three-year-old Onasakenrat was asked to become chief of his people. He was the first Mohawk chief who knew how to read and write.

His new skill gave "Chief Joseph" the ability to discover, through reading government and church documents, the extent of the false dealings between the Catholic church and the Mohawks. When he eagerly threw himself into the task of leading his people, his first priority was to reclaim the seigneury lands for the Mohawks.

Feeling betrayed by their former protege, the Sulpician priests fought back, with support from the federal government in the new nation of Canada. It was just a year after confederation.

Chief Joseph pursued the battle, warning the Sulpicians in 1869 that they had eight days to leave the mission. For his efforts, he was arrested at three o'clock in the morning, along with three other Mohawks. They were released on the promise to keep the peace and obey the "law of the land."

Added to the conflict was a growing influence by Methodist missionaries, who were more sympathetic to the Mohawks' land claims and less restrictive than the Catholics. Chief Joseph himself had abandoned the Catholic church and become a Methodist minister, and by 1869 most of the Mohawks had left the Catholic church in favor of the Methodists.

Chief Joseph was sentenced to six months in jail for claiming a larger tract of land for his personal use than the Sulpicians had stipulated. Many other Mohawk men were jailed between 1870 and 1873, simply for refusing to ask permission from the Sulpicians to use land.

By 1875 European settlers were also well established in the area, especially in the village of Oka, which was incorporated as a municipality. The influx of more and more people left the Mohawks confined to smaller and smaller pieces of land. Chief Joseph was jailed a second time in 1876, again for using a piece of land without Sulpician permission.

The conflicts that ensued over the years became a complex tangle that pitted government against Mohawks and Catholics against Protestants, with Mohawks and whites on both sides.

Chief Joseph died in 1881 at the age of thirty-five, after attending a banquet in Montreal hosted by the Sulpician order. The cause of death was given as food poisoning.

But before he died, besides leading his people in the fight for land, Chief Joseph had given them another gift. Faced with months at a time in jail, he used the opportunity to translate the four Gospels into the Mohawk language.

※◆◆◆◆◆◆◆◆※

It was early July, 1990. Since March 10, Mohawks had been occupying The Pines, a seventy-hectare piece of land, to prevent the municipality of Oka from taking it over for a planned expansion of a nine-hole golf course. As long as they occupied The Pines, they reasoned, the bulldozers would not come in and mow down the trees.

But the atmosphere was heating up, and rumors were circulating that the Sûreté du Quebéc were going to come in and take over The Pines by force.

The Mohawks had been given till July 9 to obey a court injunction to take down the barricade at the entrance to The Pines. That day, Quebec's minister for Indian Affairs, John Ciaccia, asked Oka's mayor, Jean Ouellette, to postpone the golf course expansion. Ouellette remained intransigent. The Mohawks refused to leave The Pines.

On July 11, the SWAT team moved in.

Women are traditional keepers of the land in Mohawk culture; their job is to make sure the land is there for the coming seven generations. Mohawk men are warriors, or, according to tradition, Rotiskenrakete, "carriers of the burden of peace." So when the SQ arrived, it was the women camping in the woods who came forward from where they were making breakfast in The Pines, and confronted the police.

What happened that morning shook everyone. Police charged into The Pines, shots were fired, hand grenades thrown, police and warriors clashed in the woods, women and children ran for cover through the tear gas, and an SQ officer, thirty-one-year-old Corporal Marcel Lemay, was fatally wounded.

The panic and confusion in the forest that morning only made the conflict worse. No one admitted to having shot at Lemay. The Mohawk warriors, who had a heavy cache of arms, insisted they had not killed Lemay, and that they had not been the first ones to fire. The SQ swore they had only shot bullets into the air, not at people. But when the forest cleared, there were bullet holes in the trees. They had been shot from the SQ side, and they were chest high, knee high and head high.

Hearing about the gun battle, Mavis and one of her nieces got on the phone to pray for the people in the forest. Meanwhile, the wind changed and the tear gas came back in the faces of the SQ officers. The SQ fled on foot to Oka, leaving several patrol cars behind.

"So our men took the vehicles and put them across the road

with a tree so they couldn't come back," says Mavis. The original barrier, a small mound of dirt, was now a serious barricade on Highway 344 near the treatment center.

On Sunday, July 15, Mavis Etienne was hosting the Mohawk Gospel Program on CKHQ when she received word that there was to be a community planning meeting at the gym that evening. Mavis announced the meeting on her program, and after her shift was over, headed to the gym, where she and another individual were chosen as negotiators to try and settle the dispute peacefully.

The summer of 1990 proved to be one of the most difficult and tense in modern Canadian history. For seventy-eight days, the Mohawks stood face to face with the SQ, then the Canadian Armed Forces, refusing to give up their piece of land. Sympathetic Mohawks in Kahnawake, south of Montreal, blocked a major bridge in support. The whole area was full of tension. The people of Chateauguay, on the other side of the Mercier bridge, lost access to Montreal. Clashes between Mohawks and whites, and amongst whites, ensued.

And in Oka, not all of the town's eighteen hundred residents wanted to see the golf course doubled. Many felt the mayor, Jean Ouellette, was making his own decisions without consulting with the people.

Negotiations with the government were futile. "They were trying to treat us like we were all terrorists," Mavis recalls. "But we were professionals. They were trying to justify why they sent the Army of Canada around the Mohawk land."

The treatment center, dubbed the TC, became the Mohawks' headquarters throughout the standoff. For forty-seven of the seventy-eight days, Mavis continued to go in to the TC, despite protests from her husband. "He was so afraid they were going to shoot us," she says. At that point the Army was still on the outskirts of the community, but she knew they were planning to move in closer.

The Armed Forces had brought in twenty-six hundred troops to replace the thousand SQ officers, erecting their own barricades to prevent the movement of people in and out of The Pines. As the summer wore on, the Army moved closer and closer in. The barbed-wire barricade got smaller and smaller. Mavis promised her husband that if the Army came too close, she would leave the TC and go home, a few miles away, in order to be on the same side of the barricade as he was.

Mavis and James Etienne were approaching their twenty-fifth wedding anniversary on July 17 that summer. A big celebration was planned for July 14, the Saturday before. Rycki had invited fifty people to come to the party. But when the crisis started, the celebration was canceled. It was never rescheduled.

Despite the constant tension, people used humor to lighten the atmosphere. Once a soldier called the TC to talk to a particular person, and whoever answered the phone challenged him:

"First you have to answer three questions," he said. "Number one, what's Wayne Gretzky's number?

"Number two, what are the names of the Three Stooges?

"Number three, what's the Army of the Government of

Canada doing on our territory?

"You don't know the answer? Then you can't talk to him!"

With Army flares going off in the middle of the night, helicopters buzzing overhead constantly and tanks everywhere, the summer of 1990 was mayhem. One time Mavis and other negotiators were meeting in a bus. A tank was situated nearby with its barrel aimed right at the bus. Mavis yelled at the soldiers. "You don't have to aim it right at us!" she said.

Sometimes the Army would park their tanks on someone's private property without asking. When they parked a tank on her brother's yard, Mavis phoned the Army. "Move that tank today," she ordered them.

There was only one time when she was afraid. Word was circulating that the Army tanks were moving in, and the people were warned to stay out of sight. Some were encouraged to leave Kanehsatake if they were afraid.

"I said, where am I going to go? Because this is my home."

One night before the tanks rumbled in Mavis and her family went to the basement of their home to sleep, wanting to stay away from the big upstairs windows.

But she was lying there, unable to sleep. Finally she went back upstairs. "All this time I'm saying God is in control, so what am I doing in the basement?" she asked herself.

"I came upstairs and slept like a baby, right on the couch in front of the window."

It was a Sunday in August when Mavis and Rycki decided to leave the territory to fetch food and gas. All summer the Army had been playing games with the food supply, promising they would not use food as a weapon and then turning away trucks filled with groceries.

It was the first time she had attempted to leave the territory. An Army officer stopped her at the barricade, looked in her trunk and asked to see her papers.

Mavis was aggravated. "Make sure you put everything back where you got it," she told him.

The soldier gave Mavis her papers back and apologized. "I'm sorry," he told her.

"They were just baby-faced boys," Mavis recalls. "They didn't want to be there."

After she was allowed to pass the Army checkpoint, she was stopped again by the SQ. Two burly police officers got out of their unmarked car and headed to the side where Rycki was sitting and ordered him out of the car.

Pretending to assume Rycki might be a warrior, they told Mavis they were arresting him. In fact, Rycki had nothing to do with the standoff. "My son wouldn't pick up a gun," says Mavis. "He's a peaceful person."

But it didn't take long to figure out the police were more interested in her than they were in Rycki anyway.

"Mrs. Etienne, you're under arrest," one of the officers told her.

"What are the charges?" she asked.

The police said they were arresting her for intimidation, and for being at the barricade on July 11. But she hadn't been anywhere near the barricade on the morning of July 11. "I was at home praying with my niece." It was only after she had been selected as a negotiator that she went to the barricade.

Besides, she told the officers, if they were going to arrest her for being at the barricade, they would have to arrest federal Indian Affairs minister Tom Siddon, Quebec Indian Affairs minister John Ciaccia and Quebec Chief Justice Alan Gold, who had been appointed as a special mediator. They had all been at the barricade.

The picture the police had as "proof" of her involvement in the conflict, which was taken much later than July 11, was of herself and the head of the International Federation of Human Rights, whom she had escorted to the disputed zone. So if they were going to arrest her, they would have to arrest him too, she informed them.

Mavis spent five hours at the police station and was not allowed to see her lawyer. She wrote out her testimony of what she was doing on July 11, and finally the police let her go.

After that the police harassed her every time she tried to pass the barricade, searching her car for contraband cigarettes and demanding she show them her papers. Exasperated, she began to tell them off. "I told them to get a life and to put it in their computer that I didn't sell cigarettes or use them."

After forty-seven days of going to the TC, Mavis decided it was time she stayed home. The encircling Army was coming too close, and she realized she would have to keep her promise to her husband so she wouldn't get caught on the wrong side of the barricade.

Yet she was still tempted. "I almost went back to the treatment center," she remembers. "Had I done that, I would have been caught in that circle that got closed."

✵✵✵✦✵✵✵✦✵✵✵

The conflict escalated throughout the summer. On August 28, a convoy of seventy-five vehicles was being evacuated from the community of Kahnawake, south of Montreal, where every exit was marked by angry mobs throwing rocks. A seventy-seven-year-old French Canadian man was hit in the chest by a huge rock that came crashing through the back window of the car being driven by his daughter. A week later a seventy-one-year-old Mohawk man, traumatized by the mobs, died of a heart attack in a Montreal hospital.

The standoff continued throughout September. Talks had gotten nowhere. There was tension among the Mohawks themselves and disagreement about how, or whether, to continue. Finally the people in The Pines reached a consensus. On September 26, after seventy-eight days, the Mohawks—thirty men, sixteen women and six children—walked out of The Pines. It was not a surrender.

Nevertheless, after a violent attack by the Army patrol, dozens were arrested and charged with criminal acts from rioting and obstruction of justice to assaulting peace officers. Police beat several of the warriors, demanding to know who killed Corporal Lemay. Most Mohawks were eventually released, but a few of the leaders served jail terms.

It was a costly summer. Almost four thousand Army and police troops—more than those who went to the Gulf War, Mavis points out—were deployed to fight a handful of Mohawks. Though only two lives were lost, hundreds of men, women and children suffered severe emotional trauma during the crisis. The standoff cost the Canadian government $155 million. The events were recorded by fifteen hundred journalists from around the world. The summer remains etched in every Mohawk's memory. "It's a big nightmare that you hope you'll wake up from," Mavis comments.

Though Mayor Ouellette abandoned his plans to expand the golf course that year, the dispute over the land was never resolved.

"For years I was mad at golf," Mavis says wryly. Still, she realized it was greed rather than golf that was at fault. An avid golfer, she has made it her policy never to play at Oka. "It would make a nice burial ground for the Mohawks, since it is our land," she observes.

※◇◇※◇◇※◇◇※

There were some good things that followed the crisis of 1990. A gathering called Christ Across the Cultures took place in

Chateauguay, and on the last evening of the weekend, about three hundred French people came to the church bringing baskets of food. There was a great time of fellowship and a wonderful feeling of reconciliation among those who met.

Some time after the gathering a minister from Chateauguay, where angry French Canadians had burned a Mohawk in effigy, invited Mohawk Christians to lead a native awareness weekend at his church. Mavis and her sisters sang in Mohawk and answered questions from the church people. Although some church members indicated by their body language and expressions that they were still antagonistic, they listened and over the next few days changed their views of Mohawks. Like many white people, Mavis observes, some had never even met a native person.

After that Mavis did other presentations in Chateauguay schools. Tensions have since lessened between whites and Mohawks. "The more people know," Mavis points out, "the less they're threatened."

The battle of 1990 has instilled more pride in native nations, Mavis adds. Other natives in Canada have seen how the Mohawks stood up for their land and have gained strength.

When she first started hosting the Mohawk Gospel Program, Mavis thought there were only the four Gospels in Mohawk, which were the books that had been translated by Chief Joseph

Swan when he was in jail. Then she found out that almost the entire New Testament, except for II Corinthians, had been translated into Mohawk.

Desiring to see her people reading more Scriptures in their own language, in 1999 Mavis became the coordinator of a project to complete translating the Bible into Mohawk with the help of experts from Wycliffe Bible Translators, Canadian Bible Society and World Vision Canada. But it was a team of Mohawks themselves, including Mavis, who undertook the actual translating. Some of the translators were in their seventies and eighties; all were extremely motivated to see the Bible in Mohawk. Although she had been translating choruses since she was a young adult, Mavis had always used phonetic translation methods. As part of the project, Mavis took a course in orthography, learning the correct, or at least standardized, spelling of the language.

Working with Hebrew, Greek, and several English translations of the Bible, the team painstakingly translates every chapter into Mohawk, then back-translates into English to see if the meaning is still correct. As with any translation, there are obstacles: how do you translate a word like "camel," for example, when "camel" doesn't exist in the Mohawk language? The translators got around the obstacle by describing the animal rather than coming up with another name for it. The fact that Mohawk is a very descriptive language makes it easier to do that.

Working with Mohawk Scriptures has opened a whole new world for Mavis and her brother and sister Mohawk believers. One day she decided she was going to start praying in her first language.

"I started praying in Mohawk and thanking God for sending His son to die on the cross. When I prayed in my own language the tears came to my eyes." Even though she has been fluent in English all her life, she finds special meaning in worshiping and reading in Mohawk. "When I pray about Jesus being nailed to the tree in my own language, I have had tears in my eyes because I was really able to see it."

She's especially grateful that the translation team is leaving a legacy for Mohawk readers in generations to come. "It's so exciting," she enthuses. "Serving Christ is just so exciting."

She considers the Mohawk Bible translation project a lifelong endeavor. As each book of the Bible is completed, it will be published individually. But she doesn't have to wait for the Scriptures to be published to use them to share the gospel. The project is the continuation of a legacy, one that was started by young Chief Joseph Swan when he was in prison many years ago, and continued by Mavis's mother, Susan Cree, when she translated gospel songs into Mohawk during Mavis's childhood and teen years.

Ten years after the Oka Crisis, in the summer of 2000, the mellow voice of Mavis Etienne speaks across the airwaves of the Mohawk Gospel Program on a Sunday afternoon, giving greetings, dedicating songs and inviting listeners to enjoy the gospel music and Scripture portions read in Mohawk. There's no hint of the tension there was a decade earlier. For now, there's peace in Kanehsatake.

Translated by Susan Cree

Sa ia ner nonen ten tia to re ta nion

Sa snon sa tsi nahoten ne ioson

Tsion wen tia te oh tsito ne ka ra kwa

Sa shats ten sera a kwe io ne nes ton

(Chorus)

Eh to ne niio ten ke ri wa kwe

Io ne ra kwa sa shats ten sera

iah tak kwe ni na kwe a kat tro ri

Tsi ni ios kats ne sa sen na

Nien kat ka toh na kwe kon non wen tia ke

Saht ka wen na ho ten n'io ne ra kwa

sah ni kon ra a kwe kon ne ka ha wi

She nes ton tsi ti sari wa ie re

HELEN FRANCIS

An Adventure of Her Own Choosing

"I wonder what it's like," Helen thought to herself from her perch in a tree, "to fly through the air."

In that split second she had two options: jump to the ground, or go down with the tree. At the bottom was another little girl who, for some inexplicable reason, had decided to chop down the tree with Helen in it! Maybe she was trying to scare Helen. Maybe she saw her chance to get back at one of the kids who taunted her with a silly jingle.

Eight-year-old Helen stayed where she was. "I was suddenly possessed with the crazy notion to stay put and experience what it felt like to fly through the air," she recalls. When she landed with a thump, her chin jarred against the trunk. A small boy who was watching the episode pointed at her face, wide-eyed, and said *mihko*. It was the Cree word for blood.

Though she recovered from the injury, to this day she has a scar on her chin that reminds her of the time she tried to fly.

✶◈✤◈✶◈✤◈✶

Helen Francis has experienced many adventures since that day in northern Saskatchewan, not all of her own choosing. While she was a curious child, and an industrious one, she was given great responsibility for one so young.

She was born Helen Cook, the second child and first daughter of Walter and Mabel Cook, in the home of family friends in Cumberland House, northeastern Saskatchewan. Walter was of Cree and English ancestry, and made his living primarily by trapping, with some hunting and fishing to supplement; Mabel was a newcomer to the village, the daughter of immigrants from Norway and Sweden.

While Mabel loved nature and the changing seasons of the north, her marriage to Walter meant giving up some of the basic comforts she had been used to. With the birth of her children life became even more difficult. "The dire poverty that constantly clawed at and stripped away idyllic notions with which Mabel entered her marriage, left more regrets than happy memories," writes her daughter.

But for young Helen, early childhood was a mix of happy times and strong family relationships. She loved her dad's parents, Grannie and Moshoom. She enjoyed her siblings—her older brother Clifford and her younger brother Norman, who loved clowning around, especially showing off with his imitation of a grown-up puffing on a cigarette.

Helen was nicknamed "Toto," not after Dorothy's dog in *The Wizard of Oz*, but because as a young child she was somewhat addicted to the earlier version of a soother—a baby bottle nipple stuffed with a piece of cloth, and playfully called "cho-cho" by the natives . Though she gave up the habit when she was about five, the nickname stuck.

Every spring the family went upriver to a settlement on the North Saskatchewan called Big Eddy, where the men set their traps, the women cared for their families and the children amused themselves with whatever they found to do. Spring break-up, when the ice cracked open and the river began gushing, provided hours of entertainment for kids.

One spring day as Helen and a bunch of other children stood watching the huge chunks of ice floating by, one of the more daring older kids jumped onto an ice-floe and off again for a short but thrilling ride. It looked easy enough, Helen speculated. And too much fun to pass up. So she, too, made a leap for the nearest ice floe. Alas, she missed, and landed with a splash in the frigid waters.

The swift current immediately swept her under. She hadn't learned to swim yet and couldn't fight her way out of the icy depth. Fortunately, someone—she had no idea who—managed to pull her out of the river.

Soaking wet, she was more worried about getting in trouble at home than reflecting on her close call. So she bravely strolled around out of sight of the cabins until she was dry and it was safe to go home.

That night she got desperately sick. She was burning up with fever and there was no nurse's dispensary nearby. Her parents were worried. Finally her dad managed to get a confession out of her older brother, Cliff. But instead of getting punished, Helen was given a warm bed on the floor near the stove and a hot ginger drink.

Children are irrepressible and when one adventure ceased to amuse, there was always another one waiting around the corner. One time about half a dozen kids wandered into the forest away from camp. Before they knew it, the trail had disappeared and they were surrounded by an unfamiliar growth of trees.

It was too quiet. The children had all stopped talking, and realized they could no longer hear sounds from the campsite. They were lost.

Some of the smaller children began crying, while others began to run in a panic, only to stumble and fall. Somehow the older children managed to subdue the younger ones, and determined the direction in which the cabins were located.

They walked until they came to a stream and once again saw the path they had veered from.

Life was risky on the trapline. Sometimes the spring break-up was so powerful the riverbanks overflowed. Trappers often knew how to predict when there would be a flood. One year Walter Cook, knowing the river was going to be high that spring, built a platform-like structure out of poplars, on which he pitched a tent. When the sound of the ice breaking woke the family up in the middle of the night, parents and children quickly scrambled out to the platform and climbed into their tent. "It was a strange sensation to have a bed above the sound of gurgling water, and stranger still when daylight came to find ourselves perched above a lake of water where dry ground had been just a few hours before."

The family grew, and with it the hardships of life. At one point all four children in the household contracted whooping cough. One day Helen, who was about six, decided to "help" her baby brother by administering cough medicine while her mother was momentarily out of the house. She reasoned that more cough medicine would make him get better faster.

But something went wrong, baby Orvil threw up, Helen was found out and that meant trouble with Dad. Helen was indignant. Why shouldn't she get some credit? she wondered. After all, Orvil did manage to dislodge some of the phlegm that had choked him whenever he went into a coughing spasm.

Walter frequently had his hands full when it came to his first daughter. One time the family was seated in a heavily-packed canoe for the long trip back to Cumberland House after the trapping season. Little sister Lillian, who was three or four, was holding a knife. Big sister Helen, who was seven or eight, decided the knife might be fun to play with. When Lillian refused to give it up, Helen reached out, grabbed it by the handle and pulled it out of her sister's hand.

The sharp blade, used for skinning muskrats, sliced a gash through Lillian's fingers. "It was an awful thing for me to do," she admitted, "and I deserved the sound smack on the head which Dad gave me with his paddle."

Helen liked using a knife. One time, after watching her father clean the fat off a pelt that was stretched across a frame, Helen decided to try it herself when he stepped outside. Picking up the knife she tried to copy his procedure. To her horror, when she cut what she thought was a small piece of fat, she realized too late that she'd slit the skin, causing a flaw that would lessen its worth.

But Helen's sometimes misguided attempts at helping eventually brought her a useful skill. When her father brought home a couple of muskrats that had started to decompose due to a delay in checking the traps, she convinced him to let her have a go at skinning them instead of discarding them, and selling them herself to a trader. "I was more than happy to endure the repulsive odor just to see how large the pelts would be."

She was kept going by the thought of how much candy she could buy with the money the two pelts would bring in. And they did—a dollar-fifty for each pelt! But Helen, always the responsible one, spent a dime on candy and gave the rest to her dad.

In the Cree culture, it was common for grandparents to take over the raising of a child. Through a mutual agreement, a child, most often a male, would begin spending more and more time at his grandparents' home. A gradual adoption would take place while the child was being cared for by the grandparents. Then, once the bonding had taken place, the child remained with the grandparents. Thus Helen's brother Norman went to live with Grannie and Moshoom.

But his life with them was short. One day the news came that he had died. Though the circumstances were unclear to seven-year-old Helen, she vividly remembers witnessing her mother's deep grief. "The sight of my mother with her entire body convulsing with sobs was indelibly etched on my child's mind." It was not until years later than Helen, poring over material in the Saskatchewan Archives, learned that her brother had died of diphtheria.

⬥⬥⬥⬥⬥

In 1940, when Helen was nine, the Cooks moved west to northern British Columbia, where Mabel's elderly parents lived and where it seemed like there might be a better prospect of Walter making a living to support his family. By then there were six kids.

Accustomed to travelling by canoe, the family of eight packed themselves into a car with Mabel's brother-in-law,

Uncle Bert, who was the driver, to make the trek from Nipawin, Saskatchewan, to Sweetwater, B.C., a journey of several days.

The new chapter of their life was marked with difficulty from the start. Helen clearly remembers her first meeting with her mother's sister, Aunt Ellen. Larger, louder and coarser than Mabel, Ellen took one riveting look at Helen and exclaimed, "Gawd, but you look just like Clara!"

Clara was her adopted daughter, who had run away as soon as she was old enough after being ill-treated by her adoptive mother.

Though they didn't live in the same house, the two families clashed, largely due to Ellen's disdain for and resentment of Walter, who she thought wasn't a good enough provider for her sister.

Up until that time, Helen had not attended school. Attendance was not enforced in Cumberland House in those days, and Helen, being terrified of school, refused to go. Her parents hadn't made her go because an academic education wasn't seen as important for the kind of life they lived. Children learned the skills they needed for survival by working with their families and communities.

But that year in B.C., both Helen and Cliff started school, advancing from first grade to third grade in one year. She and Cliff enjoyed school and did well. In spelling bees they were usually put on opposite teams, and more often than not, they were the only two left standing at the end, the others having been disqualified.

Although the other kids were white, Helen doesn't recall feeling out of place at school, except for being the victim of one older boy's taunts. He took to calling her "stupid," and never let up, even after he dropped out of school.

One incident from those days in northern B.C. stands out like none other. The war was on, and the American army had built camps near Dawson Creek. Often Helen and Cliff would hitch a ride the seventeen miles into Dawson Creek, which was bigger than Sweetwater, for something different to do.

On one of these trips the siblings got separated, and Helen, who was eleven or twelve, found herself making her way home alone. She passed by a checkpoint booth near the army barracks, hoping to see her brother waiting for her, and when she didn't, continued down the road to hitch-hike.

It was dusk. Out of sight of the checkpoint she saw two figures running across the field toward her. Thinking one of them might be Cliff, she waited.

They were soldiers. Helen spun around and started running back to town. One of the men grabbed her around the waist and started to drag her to the ditch. The other watched the road.

Panicking, Helen fought back, scratching and kicking until sheer adrenalin set her free. She managed to escape from the men and take off down the highway. When she finally got home that night, she didn't tell a soul about her encounter. But she knew then that childhood was over, and life wasn't going to be as carefree as it used to be.

During the three years in Sweetwater, Walter Cook struggled

to make a living. At one point he went further north to work on the Alaska Highway, which meant separation from the family for long periods of time. Years later Helen's younger sister Margaret, while going through their father's papers after he died, found a letter Helen had written to her dad. In it she had updated him on all the major progress and events of the family. Her dad had kept that letter without her knowing, a gesture which told his daughter that he loved and cared about his family more than he had ever been able to express.

Walter Cook missed the trapping life, and eventually gave up his job on the highway and returned to trapping, with poor results. He caught very little, which further infuriated his sister-in-law. One day Ellen confronted Walter on the road, clutching an axe in her hands, and threatened to kill him. Walter didn't flinch. He just stood there and calmly said, "Go ahead."

Helen stood watching with a mix of fear and pride: afraid that her father would be wounded or killed; proud of him for not showing any fear himself, or fighting back.

Fortunately, Ellen didn't follow through with the threat.

But life was too hard, and Walter missed his home. After three years of growing tension, he announced that he was moving back to Saskatchewan, and he was taking some of his children with him. It wasn't the first time he had threatened to leave. The marriage had become one of conflict, and there were already signs that Mabel had taken an interest in someone else. This time, Walter was determined to make good on his threat.

Accustomed to making his own moccasins, he got out a couple of bolts of cloth and hand-sewed new dresses for his three daughters to wear on the trip. Despite his lack of experience in sewing clothes, the dresses turned out fine.

Meanwhile, Mabel went to Dawson Creek to report her husband to the police. While she was gone, Walter, with Helen, Lillian, Herman, and Margaret—who was just 15 months old—walked away from the shack that had been their home to hitch a ride on the highway to Dawson Creek, where they would board the train. Cliff stayed behind, standing forlornly on the dusty road watching them go until they turned a bend, wishing he could go too. But because he was old enough to work and earn money, his mother needed him to stay.

Family life as she had known it had ended, and twelve-year-old Helen now had the responsibility of caring for her younger siblings. But she was excited to be going back to her home in Cumberland. She had forgotten her Cree language while in B.C., but returning to Cumberland meant relearning it well enough to converse again.

<hr />

Life back in Cumberland House meant hard work, including scrubbing laundry on a washboard in a galvanized tub. Grannie, the matriarch, was needed on the trapline. Moshoom had since died.

When she reached her fifteenth birthday, just before she

completed grade seven, Helen quit school, believing she was too old to be sitting in a classroom when there were more important things to do. Besides her younger siblings to care for, a child welfare worker asked her to also care for three young cousins who had been neglected. That arrangement, which was supposed to be short-term, lasted a year. She did her best. "I was capable of keeping them clothed, fed and clean," she writes, "but beyond that I could not provide the nurturing only a mother can give."

At fifteen, Helen wanted her own trapline. She wasn't old enough to get her own licence but she was able to get one under her father's name. She and her older cousin Ruby shared a dozen traps, making their rounds twice a day to check. They did well that season, with Helen snagging close to a hundred pelts. Later she became her dad's skinner, deftly removing the fur from the animals. By the following year she was an expert, working from morning till night. In that season she skinned a record 1,200 muskrats for her dad and another 600 for another trapper.

When Lillian was ten she was injured in a fall. After she spent a lengthy time in the hospital, the nurse caring for her, Miss Scriver, announced she wanted to adopt Lillian rather than send her home. Walter Cook didn't want to lose his daughter, but he lost custody when Miss Scriver contacted Mabel and received signed permission to take Lillian. Walter realized it was futile to argue with the authorities. Even though he knew in his heart that he was a good and caring father, who would take the word of a Cree trapper over that of a white woman?

Attending church was never more than a routine—although the Cook children had been christened in an Anglican church the family seldom attended—but one Sunday morning when she was almost eighteen, following a burst of inspiration, Helen used church as an excuse for something that at the time seemed far more important. There was a new young man in town, and Helen wanted to meet him.

Dressing in her finest and soliciting the help of her cousin Ruby, already married, Helen made her way to the Anglican Church, which was conveniently situated beyond a provincial government building where employees from the Department of Natural Resources (DNR) lived and worked. One of them was the new field officer people had told her about, a nice young Cree fellow named Tom Francis.

Casually the two young women dropped in to say hello and welcome the young man to town and check him out. The brief meeting was disappointing to Helen. Tom didn't show any interest in her. He only talked to his superior about garden seeds!

The reserved field officer, however, was more interested than he let on. He had already spotted Helen in the Hudson's Bay store and confessed to her later that he was smitten from the start. A while after that first meeting, mellowed by a few drinks at a community dance, Tom swung Helen around the dance floor and charmed her with his wit.

There was definitely a mutual attraction. But there was a

slight obstacle. Helen's Grannie was at the dance, too, as her chaperone. Never mind. Tom gallantly offered to walk both the ladies home. Grannie was almost blind by then, and Tom gave her his arm to guide her over the dark and uneven ground.

Grannie, however, was more accustomed to the terrain than he was. She could tell by touch where she was. Tom, on the other hand, stubbed his toe on a rock. "Yo-ho, Grannie," he quipped in Cree. "I have met a rock." As Tom was not fluent in Cree—he had not been allowed to speak his native language in residential school—his effort made Grannie laugh and endeared him to her for the rest of her life.

Five months later, on October 4, 1949, Tommy Francis and Helen Cook were married in the small Anglican church in Cumberland. For eighteen-year-old Helen, marriage meant a change in status: she was no longer a girl nicknamed Toto; she was now Mrs. Tom Francis, the field officer's wife!

From then on, her ambition was simple: she wanted to be a mother.

✖⊘⊘✦⊘⊘✦⊘⊘✖

It was the middle of December when Tom, Helen and her cousin Ruby, by then five months pregnant, found themselves on an unexpected camping trip, not knowing where they were or how they would make it home in the freezing temperature and deep snow.

The trek had started out smoothly enough. The mission was

to fetch a Bombardier—a large vehicle with both skis and heavy wheels used for travelling over ice and snow—and bring it back from Flin Flon, Manitoba, to Cumberland House. By using a shortcut along a bush trail, the trio could make the trip home in a day's travel.

But once they entered the bush, the Bombardier's motor began to sputter and stall. Then there were fallen trees blocking the trail. The three limped along for some time, one person maneuvering the vehicle while the others removed fallen trees. When they reached a clearing they realized it was too late in the day to continue, so they built a campfire, exhausted from the day's work, ate some lunch they had brought with them and tried desperately to stay awake. Sleeping out in the open at that time of the year meant freezing to death.

In the morning, realizing the Bombardier was not going to cooperate, the three set out walking the twenty-four miles to Cumberland House. It was, Helen recalls, "the longest walk any of us had ever attempted."

Armed with a few supplies, the weary travellers grew more and more tired from the trek. Helen discarded the extra coat she had put on, feeling it too heavy. Ruby, who was especially weary from the burden of her pregnancy, could hardly keep going. When it began to get dark again and the three hit a snow squall, obliterating any visibility, Ruby began hallucinating and begged the other two to leave her behind.

"But we refused to leave her to what we knew was certain death," says Helen. "I slapped her, gingerly at first, and then harder at her own pleading. It helped to waken her from the sleepwalking state she had slipped into. She told me that she was dreaming and in her dream she was in a hotel room that had wallpaper with stars on the ceiling."

As they pushed on in exhaustion, Helen herself began to hallucinate. "Tom looked like he was skating instead of walking. And sometimes the shoreline appeared close, only to recede in the next movement in the far distance. I knew then that if we did not soon find the village we would perish."

Finally, finally, after sixteen hours of walking and no sleep for two days, at 2:30 a.m., the three stumbled into Walter Cook's house.

Four months later, Ruby gave birth to a healthy baby boy.

Less than six months after their marriage, Tom was transferred to another village, the Dene community of LaLoche in northwestern Saskatchewan. Although the transfer came with a promotion, for the young bride it meant uprooting from her beloved Cumberland House, leaving behind her trapline and family, and flying to a distant village to start a new chapter in her life.

By that time Helen was also pregnant with her first child.

❈❖❈❖❈❖❈

The new location brought many adjustments. Tom and Helen Francis now had an elevated status due to Tom's promotion to senior field officer, and they lived in a larger house than they had ever thought necessary, which even came with running water! No more hauling water in buckets. With that house also came the responsibility of hosting business people and government officials.

In September Helen flew on her own to Ile a la Crosse, where there was a hospital. There she gave birth, three weeks overdue, to baby Linda Caroline, weighing a healthy ten pounds, eight ounces.

Among the people she met in her new village were evangelical missionaries, Art and Dorothy Wellwood. When Dorothy invited her to a Sunday service in their home, Helen accepted. Though the setting was much less formal than the Anglican services Helen had been accustomed to in Cumberland House, she still sensed an aura of reverence in the Wellwoods' dining room.

"I liked Dorothy," Helen recalls, "but I sometimes had doubts about her unbiased friendliness." White people, in her experience, had always kept her at arm's length. She couldn't help but be suspicious of Dorothy's motives. And then there were the rules and regulations. Playing cards was *forbidden*, replaced by more acceptable games like crokinole and pick-up sticks; dancing and going to movies were completely out of the question.

Within that first year Dorothy Wellwood started a home Bible study for interested women in the community. Helen attended, enjoying the Bible stories she remembered from her childhood in Sunday school in Cumberland.

That year, after a Christmas trip home to Cumberland House, Tom stopped for business in Prince Albert while Helen and

Linda went back to LaLoche via Buffalo Narrows. There Helen decided to attend a small church, the Gospel Lighthouse. And there she heard a missionary deliver a powerful sermon on God's judgment. "I had the uneasy feeling that he was preaching at me," she says. Most of the congregation was made up of missionaries and their children, and a couple of Native children.

Even when she returned to LaLoche, Helen could still hear the missionary's words ringing in her ears. Then she began to dream nightly that the Lord was going to return and she wouldn't be ready to meet Him.

"One evening at dusk I was looking out over the lake from the kitchen window when I saw a bright star just above the horizon," she writes in her memoirs. "As I watched, the light changed from one color to another. I became apprehensive thinking maybe it was the Lord about to appear. It was a new experience for me to be so fearful all the time. Sure! There were those moments of fear that had a rational explanation, but this? I had no idea what was happening to me. And if somebody had told me I was under conviction I would not have understood its meaning."

Helen found herself anxious to resume Bible studies, which had stopped while the Wellwoods were away on a leave. One night after their return, following a Bible study, Dorothy Wellwood popped the question: "Have you ever thought about giving your heart to Jesus?"

"Yes, I have," was Helen's unhesitating response.

As they knelt down in Dorothy's living room, Helen, who

had never prayed before except to recite the Lord's prayer, acknowledged she was a sinner and asked Jesus to come into her heart.

Two things happened immediately: Helen felt the burden of fear lift from her heart—and the gas lamp went out! Momentarily uneasy at the thought of the gas lamp exploding, Helen then felt a wonderful peace come over her like a warm blanket. In later years Helen used the incident to describe how her soul, once in darkness, was filled with a light far more brilliant than any earthly light.

At first Tom was annoyed and sarcastic about his wife's decision. He resented "religion" after growing up in a residential school where Native children were strapped for not memorizing Scripture. But he still had a sense that there was a God.

Helen had always been short-tempered and impatient; independent and proud. Although she didn't change overnight, Tom eventually began to see some differences in her. Pride was replaced with humility and sensitivity. "My conscience was awakened to so many things that I hadn't noticed so much or was aware of," she recalls. Her short temper remained active, however, and Tom sometimes took advantage of that to remind her how un-Christian her behavior could be.

It was only a few months, though, before Tom himself gave up the fight, and asked Jesus into his own heart.

But they had much to learn about living like Christians, and in the conservative mission context of a small village in northern Saskatchewan, that meant finding out what they could or could not do. Since there was no cinema in LaLoche, it was easy to rule out movies. Nor were dances a huge temptation, since they were seldom held in the small community.

Playing cards was another matter, and Helen found it difficult to understand just why this and other activities were wrong. Later in life, as she matured in her Christian walk, she looked back and wondered if the strict teaching she received as a young Christian was too legalistic.

The missionaries, with all good intentions, "were more interested in the do's and don'ts rather than the caring and waiting for the Holy Spirit to do the convicting." Helen sometimes felt that the older Christians were "checking up" on her to make sure she was behaving properly, not playing cards and not going to movies. "I felt there were other things that were more serious in the line of wrong-doing." At times she was confused about whether she was just trying to please the missionaries with her behavior or whether she was pleasing the Lord.

Tom's biggest struggle was smoking, but he was eventually able to defeat the habit he'd had since he was a teenager.

Although they had both been baptized in infancy, Tom and Helen decided they wanted to be baptized by immersion in a lake to signify their new faith. For that they travelled up the river from Ile a la Crosse, where they now lived, to the mission at Buffalo Narrows.

Tom and Helen's decisions to live as Christians were to change the couple's life in a way they had never planned.

Helen's only goals had been to be a wife and mother. Tom was content in his work as a field officer.

Now, as young Christians, they were being pressured to consider becoming missionaries themselves.

❊❊❊❊❊❊

The missionary "call", as it was, came in the form of a question from Dorothy Wellwood. "Have you ever thought about going into full-time work for the Lord?" she asked Helen one day when she was in Ile a la Crosse for a doctor's appointment.

The young Christian immediately resisted. She and Tom had no supporting church, no family or friends to send them parcels, and besides, they weren't white. "There was nothing from our background that would support the idea that we were on an equal footing with white people", Helen reflects. The couple had only recently gained a measure of self-sufficiency that gave them a sense of responsibility. The knowledge that they were overcoming stereotypes also added to their feeling of independence and self-worth. How could they give all that up without feeling they had regressed?

Even now she wonders if the "call" came too soon. "When it comes prematurely from a too-zealous desire to produce results", she writes in her memoirs, "we can never be quite sure if the calling did come from God or not....Were we to some degree manipulated to make a decision that could have been left to a later date?"

Until then Helen's primary responsibility had been for her immediate family and her younger siblings, who lived with her on occasion. Tom had always been interested in helping his fellow Natives, however, and he responded more quickly to the thought of leaving his career behind and forsaking all for missionary work.

⬛❂✦❂✦❂⬛

As it turned out, the notion of "forsaking all" was forced on Tom and Helen when their house burned down while they were away in LaLoche in 1953. Practically all their possessions, except those few things they had with them, were gone. If that wasn't enough, Tom's employer and the owner of the house, the DNR, refused to compensate the couple for the loss.

Whether it was God's doing or not, the fact that they no longer had a home of their own hastened the couple's decision to go to Bible school in preparation for mission work. Tom resigned from his secure position with the DNR and the couple chose Mokahum Indian Bible School in Cass Lake, Minnesota, for their studies.

Despite the criticism that accompanied their decision to head into the unknown, Helen found strength in Jesus' words in Matthew 6:25, 32 and 33: *Take no thought for your life, what ye shall eat, or what ye shall drink; nor yet for your body, what ye shall put on...for your heavenly Father knoweth that ye have need of all these things...But seek ye first the Kingdom of God and His righteousness, and all these things shall be added unto you.*

When she looked at it that way, it was actually exciting to be embarking on a new adventure, this time with God as her guide.

At Cass Lake, Helen's eleven-year-old sister Margaret, who was living with them at the time, was enrolled in the local elementary school, while three-year-old Linda stayed with a babysitter so her mother could attend classes.

Helen enjoyed studying, but being shy and lacking confidence, she dreaded standing up in front of the class. She also found it hard adjusting to the social activities that were part of college life. The games seemed too childlike and undignified. Though still in her early twenties, Helen had already had far more responsibility than most people her age. Looking back, she feels she grew up too fast. "I never had a chance to enjoy my teen years like a lot of others do." Besides, some of the games went contrary to behavior that had been deemed appropriate where she grew up. Perhaps there was a cultural difference between Natives who grew up in remote northern areas and those who came from the south.

The next summer, Tom was offered a job in Ile a la Crosse with the Saskatchewan Agricultural department, encouraging Natives to plant their own gardens. The position came with one proviso: He was not allowed to preach on the job.

Between his income, living frugally and gifts from supportive Christian friends, Tom and Helen were able to save enough money to return to Minnesota for a second year of Bible school training. By the end of that academic year, however, they believed God wanted them to spend the following summer in ministry. Through Northern Canada Evangelical Mission they ended up in northern Alberta, where Tom did the work of an evangelist—enabling him to preach on the job!—and Helen kept the household going.

Because the work was unpaid, by the fall of 1955 they had little money to provide for their third and final year at Bible school. But they were learning to trust in God for their needs, and God did indeed provide, sometimes in unexpected ways.

En route back to Minnesota, the family stopped in Saskatoon, where little Linda came down with the measles, which delayed their departure from the city. An acquaintance there arranged both for a place to stay and for Tom and Helen to give their testimonies at a Sunday service. The congregation took up an offering and gave it to the young family. Helen was overwhelmed with their demonstration of love and concern at the service, which might never have happened if Linda hadn't contracted measles!

Other, similar incidents took place as well, giving Tom and Helen the money they needed to see them through the rest of their schooling. And some of the contacts they made in Saskatoon became long-term supporters.

The pair graduated from Bible school in Cass Lake in the spring of 1956, but not before another test. Less than a month before graduation, Tom was diagnosed with tuberculosis and sent to a sanitarium in another town for recovery. The news scared Helen. She worried that she would lose Tom, and the thought of living without him made her feel, for the first time in her life, truly abandoned.

That's when the college president stepped in. He and the Bible instructor, convinced there was a way around Tom's hospital "sentence," talked Tom into signing himself out of the sanitarium, against objections from the hospital staff. He spent the rest of the term in bed in the couple's dorm suite, while Helen continued to attend classes and shared her notes with her confined husband.

Meanwhile, concerned that they had let go of a very sick man, hospital staff visited the Mokahum campus and made sure Tom got another X-ray. That X-ray showed a mere shadow of what had been there before.

He was healed.

❊❊❊ ❊ ❊❊❊ ❊ ❊❊❊

The couple's first assignment as missionaries with the NCEM was as relief workers in Buffalo Narrows, northern Saskatchewan. Besides the hard physical work of looking after a large garden left by the previous missionaries, Helen now had to cope with the nausea brought on by pregnancy. Linda, who was about to start school, was going to have a sibling.

In the fall, the family moved to Big River, where NCEM was starting a Bible school. It was in a temporary location at a summer camp, and there were just five students. But it was a start. Tom taught in the Bible school, while Helen kept her role of providing meals—three students ate with them—and looking after her family, which again included her sister Margaret. When the term ended, they moved to Meadow Lake, where NCEM headquarters were located.

Tom and Helen's lives as evangelist-missionaries meant going where there was a need, often living in temporary or cramped quarters. It also meant separation, as Tom was required to fly out on evangelistic trips, leaving his family behind. During the winter of 1957, when Tom was conducting meetings in northern Ontario, Manitoba and Saskatchewan, Helen, by that time seven months pregnant, chopped wood to keep the family warm with an old-fashioned wood stove. Though her extended stomach made chopping challenging, she remembers preferring that task to the monotony of doing dishes or scrubbing the floor.

That winter Helen gave birth to Ross Timothy (Tim), whom Tom rushed home to visit briefly before resuming his evangelistic work in a small northern community.

Later that year the Francis family ended up in Round Lake (now called Weagamow Lake), a remote village in northern Ontario, where they were greeted warmly by the Saulteaux people. Though poor, they were hospitable.

After nine months in Round Lake, the family moved once again to Meadow Lake. But this, too, was a temporary arrangement. Their next move, in 1959, was to The Pas, Manitoba, where Helen had spent some of her time growing up. It was a move she looked forward to, since she was familiar with both the community and the people.

Alas, the five years in The Pas turned out to be the most wretched in her life. Everything seemed to come crashing in on her. She went through the motions of caring for her children and husband, but inside she was sinking into depression. The Pas no longer had that exciting, carefree atmosphere she had sensed as a child. Now she was an adult, with children of her own, saddled with a constant round of work.

Then there was racism, which came in the form of comments, children taunting and chasing other children, and other minor but malicious actions, like drivers deliberately splashing a Native pedestrian.

The Pas is still like that, Helen reflects. With Natives and non-Natives living in close proximity, many of the non-Natives have developed stereotypes that aren't easily let go. Even Natives who are Christians are assumed to be "drunk, irresponsible Indians."

And when Helen's Grannie died of a stroke, it marked the end of an era, in which Grannie had been matriarch, chaperone and stabilizing influence in the Cook family.

When Tom was away, Helen tried to build a social sphere by attending a monthly women's group. But even there, where women represented various social backgrounds and professions, she felt out of place. "I was like a misfit in the new world and an alien in the old."

She had to admit it: like Moses and the children of Israel,

she was wandering in the wilderness. She was lonely, isolated, underappreciated, and lacking in the joy of the Lord. She dreaded having devotions, because there didn't seem to be any way she could follow the scriptural model of a joyful Christian life.

"But somehow I knew, deep down inside, that God held the answer to my need." In desperation, she began to call out to Him, asking Him to show her a way out of the mire. Why was she plagued with feelings of unworthiness and failure?

One day in 1962 she received a letter from a retired pastor who wrote simply to encourage her and Tom. As she was reminded that God knew the struggle she was going through, the words were like a balm on her heart.

She began to spend more time in prayer, and in the quiet of a morning, she sensed in a way she had never sensed before the presence of the Lord. "It was warm, it was peace, and it was all around me for I'm not sure how long." She soaked in God's healing presence for some time.

After that she found something changed. The Bible came alive, and she could hardly wait to read it each day. The words spoke of joy, peace and abundant life rather than condemnation. And the drudgery went out of her daily work! She was able to approach even the most mundane tasks with joyfulness.

And in good time: she now had a third child, Debbie, to care for. A light sleeper, Debbie required frequent attention from her mother, who was also nursing her. Helen's newfound energy and joy gave her what she needed to cope.

The following years brought more moves and another child. Terri was born in 1965—a fourth child and a third daughter. By that time the Francis family was living near Prince Albert, Saskatchewan, where the NCEM headquarters were now located. The house provided for them to live in was lovely but once again too crowded, so Tom set about building a more suitable one, with the help of a couple of volunteer builders, a donation for the property and a low-interest loan for the purchase of building supplies.

Despite the family's good fortune, Helen struggled. All her life she had worked hard; all her life she had tried her best to make things perfect for those she was given the responsibility to care for. The small house, the building project, the extra workers to feed—all added up. But by pushing beyond her strength—just as she, Tom and Ruby had done during that long, freezing walk to Cumberland House, and just as she had done many times in her childhood and youth—she overextended herself, this time with physical and emotional consequences.

Her milk dried up overnight when Terri was only six weeks old, for example; and one restless night, too tired to sleep, it seemed like she left her body and looked down on it from above the bed. Years later she read a book that explained the out-of-body experience is caused by something that is beyond the body's ability to handle.

Helen had always been wary of the effect of drugs or

alcohol—drinking had never interested her—so she refused to consult a doctor, knowing she would likely be prescribed some kind of medication. Instead she turned to the Great Physician. "I clung desperately to the God who had so wonderfully revealed His presence to me three years before in The Pas."

There was no instant relief, but between her tenacity in clinging to her relationship with God and moments when the oppression would lift and sun shine into her life, Helen survived. Those were moments when Scripture verses would come to her, unbidden. One of the verses was Luke 22:31—"Satan has desired to have you that he may sift you as wheat. But I have prayed for you that your faith fail not."

How wonderful it was to hear the words Jesus had said to Peter. "The idea that Jesus prayed for me braced me as nothing else could have done."

Helen especially struggled when Tom went away on his frequent trips to evangelize in isolated communities and disciple new believers. His absence meant the greater parenting responsibility fell to his wife, who, despite years of looking after children, still felt inadequate. "I felt I didn't really have a role model in my mother," she points out. Her mother had often been sick, tired, or seemingly disinterested in her children. Then, of course, Helen had taken on parenting responsibilities herself when she was just twelve. From that time on she had no mother of her own caring for her.

Now, as missionaries, the couple had greater expectations placed on them, both as Christians and as parents. Because Tom was away so much, Helen was overly strict with her children, wanting them to grow up "in the fear and nurture of the Lord," but placing more emphasis on "fear" than "nurture."

<hr />

Tom's evangelistic zeal and his commitment to ministry brought fruit, not just on the northern reserves, but in Helen's family as well. On a visit from Cumberland House, Helen's dad responded to Tom's query about his spiritual condition and accepted Jesus as his Savior. As it turned out, that was the last time Helen saw him alive. Shortly after that, he died suddenly while building a fire in his airtight heater. Grateful that her father did not suffer in death, Helen recognized the reality of the words in I Corinthians 15: "Oh death, where is thy sting? Oh grave, where is thy victory?"

<hr />

The years went by. The Francis family spent eighteen years in Prince Albert—a record! The four children grew up and left home, starting families of their own, and in 1982 Tom and Helen moved to Vernon, British Columbia. By that time Helen's mother, married to her second husband, was living in Vancouver and suffering from cancer. Although their relationship had been strained—even nonexistent at times—Helen desired to spend time with her mother in her last weeks on earth.

Mabel had gone through her own changes and experiences over the years, and now affirmed that she, too, had faith in Jesus as her Savior. In one of her last conversations with her mother, Helen asked her if she could forgive all those whom she felt had wronged her.

"When she agreed, I led her in prayer, naming every person I knew about who had in one way or another offended her. When we got through, Mother sighed, as if in peace, and went to sleep."

The next morning, Mabel went into a coma, and three weeks later she died.

After many more months of ministering on reserves in the Okanagan area of B.C., the couple returned to Saskatchewan, moving five times in the next five years before settling in Regina.

And that was the beginning of another adventure for Helen—this time, an adventure of her own choosing.

❋❀❋❀❋❀❋

She was restless. She had spent decades as a wife, mother and caregiver, and she longed to do something else. Her life in many ways had felt fragmented, with many twists and turns. She needed something to restore a sense of being whole.

A lover of reading and writing since her early days in school in northern B.C., Helen now had the urge to do something about a growing desire to write. And to write she felt she needed first to study. Formally, she had only a grade seven education, plus the three years at Bible school.

With encouragement from her daughter Debbie, who was working in Regina, she applied for admission to the university entrance program of the University of Regina. Much to her delight she was accepted, and enrolled in the Saskatchewan Indian Federated College (SIFC), affiliated with the university. All four of her children helped in one way or another, through financial, moral and practical support.

During the next years, "I studied, and I read and I fearfully wrote exams," she says, "until I felt that I could not read another book or write one more essay for the rest of my life."

And in 1991, the year she turned sixty, and the year she became a great-grandmother, Helen Francis graduated from university with a degree in English.

It hadn't been easy. Besides the academic pressure, Helen received news in her second term that her beloved brother Cliff, her childhood companion, had died of a stroke. As adults, though their visits had been infrequent, they had remained close. "Each time I saw him I still felt the bond that had not been erased by the years or the miles of separation."

At his funeral in northern B.C., Helen grieved like she had not for either of her parents, or for her sister Shirley who had died earlier in a car accident. She mourned the missed opportunities to talk more deeply about the circumstances that had separated them in childhood.

But her brother's death and the reflection it brought gave substance to that smouldering longing she harbored. She knew she had to write her family's story, and equipped with the educational skills to tackle such a big project, now was the time.

⧫⧫⧫⧫⧫⧫

Struggle to Survive: A Metis Woman's Story was published in 1997. It took a few years of work, including many long hours of research in Saskatchewan archives and revisiting painful experiences from the past. "It's hard to write about things that are more personal," Helen admits.

But even the process of reliving some of the more difficult times in her past brought a positive outcome. "I think getting it out on paper was kind of therapeutic."

These days, living in Regina, spending time with children and grandchildren and having time to think about doing some more writing, Helen's life is a lot less stressful than the days of chopping wood and doing laundry with no running water. Yet, this survivor has a bit of nostalgia in her, perhaps a wistfulness for some of the good aspects of the past. Besides the ambition of some day writing another book, Helen has another wish: to live in a log house by a lake.

She has struggled, but she has also survived. And knowing what she is capable of, the person who once thought she could fly from a tree still has a sense of adventure in her that shouldn't surprise anyone the next time she takes on a new project.

BESSIE MCPEEK

He Goes Before

The heritage of Bessie McPeek is a tapestry that weaves together the story of an adventurous missionary who arrived in Canada from England via South America and the story of a woman who was born in the same northern community that her parents and ancestors since time unknown had also been born.

Those two people, the enthusiastic missionary and the traditional Ojibway woman, came from vastly different backgrounds.

To tell the story of Bessie McPeek is also to tell the story of her parents.

In 1923 a young, British-born Anglican missionary priest named Leslie Garrett began working at an isolated Ojibway community called Big Trout Lake. Located in northwestern Ontario, Big Trout was several hundred miles north of a town of any size. The only white people who visited the area were Hudson Bay Company employees and occasional government workers.

The lifestyle was rugged and demanding. Garrett had to haul wood, travel by dog team in winter and canoe in summer and rely on what food he could catch or trap or what the natives gave him. But he was used to a pioneering life. His father had taken his young family to a cattle ranch in Argentina when Leslie was only eight. He had grown up in a challenging environment, once almost dying from diphtheria, which took seven out of eight children of a neighbouring Indian family.

When Leslie was fifteen, the Garretts moved to Canada, settling on a farm for the next six years. As a young teenager, he told his mother that he wanted to be a missionary. At that time he was thinking of returning to South America.

But after attending Bible college in Toronto he was invited to spend the summer working among natives north of Sioux Lookout, Ontario. Then the bishop of the area asked him if he would be willing to go to Big Trout Lake, about 350 miles north of Sioux Lookout.

A large number of the Ojibway there had become Christians over the past hundred years, many of them through the forty-year ministry of a native missionary, William Dick, who had recently retired. They had the Scriptures in syllabics, an alphabet system designed by missionary James Evans, who also translated the Bible into Cree, a language related to Ojibway, in the 19th century.

Garrett's first year at Big Trout was on his own. The settlement of about a hundred tepees and tents was between the Hudson Bay Trading Post at one end of a point and a small mission church at the other.

Life there was hard, but in some ways it was simpler than it later became. When Garrett first arrived, few of the people had seen money. They traded and bartered in furs instead. The area had not yet been developed, so there was no mining or roads, no regular means of communication or transportation.

There he spent his time learning the language, visiting people and learning the way of the land. He went down south the following summer to be married, and he and his bride Mary, after a long journey by canoe and schooner, reached Big Trout Lake in September 1924, just in time to prepare for winter. Mary must have shared her husband's sense of adventure, for she was the only white, English-speaking woman for hundreds of miles around, and had to adjust to life in a simple log house with no amenities after growing up in the larger southern city of Hamilton, Ontario.

In the early years, Leslie Garrett faced many challenges. There were both physical and spiritual needs to attend to. One Christian woman asked for prayer because she had birthed and buried eleven children, and now she was pregnant again. She did not want to face the sorrow of losing yet another child. She asked the young missionary to pray. He responded by asking her to pray first. The woman poured out her heart to God. The next spring she gave birth to a healthy baby girl, who thrived, and later had children and grandchildren of her own.

Leslie and Mary Garrett had three sons before they were able to take their first and only furlough together in 1928. They returned to Big Trout in the summer of 1929, this time arriving in the first plane ever to fly into Big Trout Lake.

A year later, however, hardship struck when Mary injured her foot falling through an open trap door into the cellar. Because there was no means of getting her out of the settlement for medical help, she suffered with her injury over the winter. It wasn't until the following spring that the family was able to fly to Sioux Lookout with a mining prospector. They took the train to Hamilton, where Mary and the boys stayed with her parents while Leslie went back to Big Trout.

But later that summer of 1931 Garrett received a telegram, delivered by the same mining plane: his wife had died. Though it was too late to go to her burial, he returned to southern Ontario. After a period of mourning, he decided to visit family in England and took his three young sons with him. Altogether, he stayed out of Big Trout Lake for a year or more.

But his calling to the north was as strong as ever, so he left his children in a home for missionary children, which was close to grandparents and other family, and returned to Big Trout Lake where he labored alone for the next six years.

He established a small nursing station at Big Trout Lake so he could help the local people with some of their physical needs. The station was very basic, but the workers there could deliver babies and treat injuries and illnesses. Parents slept on the floor when their children were in for treatment. There was no government funding, and no flights to take critically ill patients to a larger center. For years Garrett himself was the official dispenser of drugs, having to discern people's needs when they asked for "maskihki"—a word simply meaning "medicine." He was also called upon to practice dentistry, and became quite proficient at pulling teeth.

One day Garrett sent word to Kasabonika, about seventy miles east, that he needed a nurse. He was wondering if Christina Anderson, whom he had met on an earlier trip and who was known for her ability in looking after sick people, would be available to help.

❖❖❖❖❖

Kasabonika was even more isolated than Big Trout Lake. When Christina—whose name was originally Kanina—was young, no white person ever visited. There was no regular trading post there. The people lived year round in tepees, covered with moss and clay in winter and with birch bark or canvas in summer.

Christina's father had died after a moose, angered by a gunshot wound, kicked him in the chest. Christina was eighteen, the eldest child at home, and had to work hard to provide for the family.

One time after a bout of stormy weather, the family was in desperate need of food. Christina went out to check the nets under the ice, finding only two small suckers. But the family had to eat, so she cut open a larger hole, put a fishing line through it and prayed that God would send her some fish to feed the hungry family.

The first bite was a skinny jack. But when she put down the hook again, she got a large fish of about fifteen to twenty pounds. This was followed by another, and another. Before she knew it, she had almost more than she could carry home.

That day the family rejoiced in God's provisions.

✖◈✦◈✖◈✦◈✖

Christina agreed to help out at the clinic and arrived just before Easter, 1937, to report for duty. Although she wasn't formally trained, she was an excellent midwife and a skilled nurse who seemed to know just what to do in emergency situations. Leslie Garrett noticed that she was not only a good worker, but she was also a pleasant person. So one day he went to talk to the matron about her.

"Could you ask Christina if she would care to marry me?" he asked the matron, an older native woman.

"You ask her yourself," was the matron's reply.

So the young missionary, in a manner that was more pragmatic than romantic, asked Christina to come outside the nursing station because he wanted to talk to her.

"Do you think you could marry me?" he asked her.

"I don't know," she replied. "I'll have to ask my family first." Although Christina's father had died, her mother was still alive; she also had four brothers and a sister. Like Leslie, Christina had also been married before, but she had lost her husband to tuberculosis and her small daughter in a canoeing accident. She had grieved deeply, perhaps never really recovering from her loss, and she chose not to talk about it.

Garrett suggested she write to her family and consult with them. Her brother Charlie, a band councillor, came and talked to Garrett, and they agreed that marriage between the two would be acceptable. The wedding took place on June 6, 1938.

A year and two days later, on June 8, 1939, with a midwife in attendance, Christina Garrett gave birth at home to the couple's first child, a daughter. They named her Bessie, after her paternal grandmother and great-grandmother.

Bessie was followed by a boy, Herbert, in 1940, and another girl, Esther, in 1944.

As the children grew, every morning and evening their parents would sit together on the floor of their little log house and sing in Cree, read the Bible and pray together.

※◇※◆※◇※◆※◇※

Bessie remembers a happy childhood with lots of homemade toys and games. The family lived in a simple log house with no running water. The only electricity was generated occasionally from a windmill. Because her father had become fluent in the Ojibway language, that was what the family spoke at home. None of the children learned English until they left the village to go to school.

Much of the children's play mimicked what the older people did. They would build their own small tepees out of sticks and an old piece of cloth and move them around from one place to another; they would catch fish from the dock, or put a net through the ice in winter. Although she had dolls, Bessie preferred playing with her cat, a compliant feline that didn't mind being tied up in a cradleboard ("tihkinakin") and wearing a bonnet! Bessie and the other kids would also harness a couple of puppies and hitch them to a sled. That was how her father travelled in winter, visiting people in other villages.

Christina Garrett was very skilled in the traditional ways. She was an exceptional bead-worker and made beautiful moccasins. She tanned moose-hide the old-fashioned way, smoking it and pulling it taut. Sometimes the whole family got involved, sitting in a circle pulling the hide. She also knew how to make a rabbit skin parka that was woven together out of strips of fur, so it had fur on both sides and kept the wearer warm. Bessie remembers having one of these. Besides the art of beading, Christina taught her daughter to make fishnets, using long wooden needles.

Christina was also a good hunter. She would go out early some mornings and shoot ptarmigan for the day's main meal. Ducks and partridges were also plentiful. And living near a lake, the family ate a lot of fish. For a special treat they would boil the small ones whole, heads and all. Cranberries, blueberries and raspberries added a good balance to the diet. Sometimes the people would pound dried, smoked fish, put it in a birch bark container with a fish-skin of oil hidden inside. Later, they would take it out, mix the oil with the powdered fish, and sometimes add a few berries and maybe add a little sugar.

Occasionally, when a beaver was given to them, Christina would clean the tail, sprinkle it with salt and put it in the oven till it was crispy. The children liked that. Another treat was when each of the children received a little sardine can of melted lard, in which they could dip a piece of bannock and spread it with some home-made jam. Bannock always tasted extra special when it was cooked outside on the fire.

When Leslie and Christina went out on the frozen lake to check their nets, they would drop the children off at a small cabin at the end of the trail to the lake. They would give them each an enamel mug filled with hot tea mixed with oatmeal, a chunk of lard and a bit of sugar to sip on while their parents were out on the ice. That was yummy! Then their parents would come back to the cabin with a toboggan loaded up with fish, to smoke, dry or fry.

Every spring the Garretts went out on the land and lived in a tent in the woods for a couple of months. Leslie Garrett would chop trees and cut them into logs for the following winter, enlisting the kids to help by peeling the bark off the logs so the wood would dry faster. Then he pulled the load to the lakeshore to await open water. Later that summer, he would make rafts out of the logs and pull them back to the village with his motor boat.

Bessie loved playing outside in the winter. It never seemed too cold, and there was no end of activity to keep the kids busy. They would hollow out tunnels in the hard-packed snow, sculpting whole rooms inside. Or they would go skiing on homemade skis, just a little longer than their shoes, curved up like a canoe at the toe and well-iced on the bottom so they would be nice and slippery. And everyone had snowshoes. Bessie's uncle would make the frames while her mother knotted the sinew together for the middle.

One year when the lake froze it was just like a smooth, gigantic piece of glass. Bessie and her friend, noticing the wind was up one day, decided they would see what it was like to sail across the ice. So they rigged a little scrap of cloth on a metal sled and got on.

Whoosh! The two girls sailed a long distance in hardly any time at all. It was fun at the time, but Bessie later wondered if maybe it could have been just a little dangerous. What if the ice had been thin in spots? They could easily have gone through. But Bessie was adventurous and loved to have fun, even when it was sometimes risky.

One year, however, Bessie's brother wasn't as fortunate as his older sister. She and Herb and others were playing on icefloes near the lake shore, as they often did in the spring. Using smaller icefloes like boats, they pushed themselves around with long poles. All of a sudden, Herb's "boat" cracked and he fell into the water. Fortunately, it was only up to his waist.

That wasn't the family's only close call. One time, when Bessie and Herb were still very small and Esther wasn't born yet, the family was travelling by canoe, with three other passengers, and the two small children sleeping under the bow of the wooden vessel, when a gale came up and waves began swamping the boat. Frantically, Christina and Leslie tossed everything they could out of the canoe and began bailing the water out. It was a frightening experience, especially for Christina, who was certain the whole family would drown. Perhaps, in the panic of the moment, she remembered the sorrow of losing her first child in a similar accident.

But God spared the family, and they were able to make it to a nearby island, where they camped and dried their belongings before setting out for home again.

✻◈◈✦◈◈✦◈◈✻

Bessie wanted to go to school. Other kids from Big Trout Lake had gone south for residential school in Sioux Lookout, and when they came back in the summer, they sported new clothes and haircuts. They could also speak English.

Now twelve, Bessie had grown up speaking only Ojibway, although her father had taught the children some correspondence lessons in English. But because her mother had married a white man, she had lost her treaty rights. That meant the children weren't eligible to go to the Indian residential school. (It wasn't until the summer of 1990 that these rights were restored and Christina and her three children were registered with the Big Trout Lake Band.)

Instead, Bessie's father took her to a public school in Sioux Lookout and found a nice home where she could board. Although she hadn't been to school before, the teachers put her in Grade 4 at the start, and after Christmas she advanced to Grade 5. She liked school, but she was lonely. Later her landlady, Mrs. Weisenberg, said Bessie didn't talk the first whole year she was there.

She realized when she moved from the secure, familiar environment of Big Trout Lake to Sioux Lookout that the world was a bigger place than she had thought it to be. And there were differences in the south. Not everyone was the same.

Because she was part Ojibway and part white, she had to think about her identity. She noticed that white people looked at natives differently and treated them differently. She had never seen or experienced prejudice before. It was hard at first. But she realized later that God makes each person different for His own special purpose.

She took comfort in the Scriptures, like verses found in Psalm 139. *For Thou didst form my inward parts; Thou didst weave me in my mother's womb. I will give thanks to Thee, for I am fearfully and wonderfully made; Wonderful are Thy works, And my soul knows it very well* (Ps. 139: 13, 14, NAS).

She was also learning English, and by the second year she was more confident. She made friends and learned how to ice skate on old speed skates her landlady found in the basement.

During her second year in Sioux Lookout, a woman in town was holding after-school Bible clubs for children. Bessie began attending and enjoyed the stories. One day the club leader was talking about how everybody had to be sure they were going to heaven when they died.

Bessie wasn't sure. She had gone to church all her life, fitting in with her parents' beliefs. She had learned the catechism and had been baptised as a baby and confirmed as a young girl. But she still wasn't sure if she was ready to die.

The leader invited anyone who wanted to ask questions to stay behind. One day, Bessie did.

"I want to make sure I'm a Christian," she told her club leader. So the two prayed together, and from that point on Bessie knew for sure that she belonged to Jesus.

Things changed then. She was eager to tell her friends about God. When the Gideons came to her school, she volunteered to help hand out Bible portions in the neighborhood. As a child, she had always enjoyed playing roles, holding imaginary classes and pretending she was a missionary or a preacher like her father. Now she began to think about it more seriously.

God also helped her when she had to face uncertain or frightening situations. One time she was babysitting two small children in Sioux Lookout when a drunken man opened the door and lurched into the house. He was huge and Bessie was scared.

What should she do? He looked like he was angry. She had the urge to run out of the house, but she knew she couldn't leave the children, who were sleeping peacefully in their beds.

"Lord, please protect us," she prayed silently. Without a doubt, she sensed God's protection.

The man, who was a relative of the people who lived there, just walked through the house and back out again. Surely the Lord had answered her prayer.

※◇※◆※◇※◆※◇※

Bessie had been going to school in Sioux Lookout for three years when her parents made a decision to join a new mission and move away from Big Trout Lake. A missionary pilot from Northern Canada Evangelical Mission, Stan Collie, had visited the area and told the Garretts of the need for missionaries in other parts of northern Canada. Leslie wondered if he should respond, but he was waiting for a sign from the Lord. That sign came in the form of a revival that broke out at Weagamow Lake, one of the villages that he served as missionary.

It was 1954. Many people were turning to God from their old ways. They would meet each other on the trails when they were out trapping or fishing and talk to each other about the Lord. "Do you know Jesus?" they would ask each other, eager to say what God had done for them and what He could do for others. People's lives changed. Many of them didn't drink or smoke any more. This caused the local Hudson Bay store to bring in a special plane to fly out the surplus cigarettes and tobacco because people had stopped buying them!

When Leslie saw this, he took it as a sign from the Lord. The Garretts left the community they had lived in for many years and moved to Meadow Lake, Saskatchewan, where the mission's headquarters was located. Bessie was fifteen by then. She didn't want to leave her familiar surroundings at Big Trout Lake, where she had spent such a happy childhood, or the school at Sioux Lookout, but she was still too young to stay behind. Her landlady in Sioux Lookout didn't want her to leave, either. She had never had children of her own, and had come to see Bessie as a kind of daughter.

The family lived in Meadow Lake only one year. Although she made friends, it was a hard year because Bessie was sick quite a bit and missed a lot of school. First she was in the hospital getting her appendix out, and then, before she was fully healed, she took a fall from a horse during spring vacation and re-injured her side.

The Garretts moved farther north and west to Loon Lake for the next two years. Then Bessie went to boarding school in Three Hills, Alberta to finish her Grade 10 before going on to Briercrest Bible Institute in Caronport, Saskatchewan.

While she was in Three Hills, Bessie drew closer to God, and learned to accept herself as the person the Lord had made her to be. There she was challenged to dedicate her life to missionary service, whatever that might mean. She wanted to do whatever she could to help others, and to encourage them, too, to realize that God has made each one and loves each one no matter who they are.

But she wasn't certain she could undertake missionary work alone. Wouldn't it be better to have a partner to work with?

❖❖❖✦❖❖❖✦❖❖❖

Besides a yearning to do missionary work, Bessie was also interested in nursing and thought about going into nurses' training. Ever since she was seventeen, she had been working part-time in hospitals whenever she could. She started at the Loon Lake hospital just after Grade 9. Later she worked in the Meadow Lake hospital, mainly on the children's ward and on maternity. There she did a variety of work, even spending a summer in the X-ray lab.

One summer when she was working in the hospital she was staying at a mission residence about a mile away from work. Because she sometimes worked till 11 p.m., she had to walk home from work late at night. One time as she was walking home she noticed a truck following her. A couple of guys were in the truck and they called out to her as they went by.

She ignored them, but inside she began to get scared. As they drove around the block to circle by her again, she prayed that God would help her know what to do. She didn't want to start running, because that would only show the guys she was afraid.

Abruptly she turned up a walk and into someone's yard as if it were her own home. She didn't know who lived there. She just felt that's what she should do. For several minutes she stood behind the house, waiting for the guys in the truck to give up and drive away. Meanwhile, she thanked God for giving her the ability to think quickly and act wisely.

✖✖✚✖✖✚✖✖

After graduating from Briercrest, Bessie went back to Meadow Lake. She was still interested in becoming a missionary, but she wasn't sure what her role should be. Perhaps she should still go into nurses' training. In the meantime, she got work at the hospital.

It was the fall of 1962. That same year, a young man from southern Saskatchewan, George McPeek, had graduated from Canadian Bible College in Regina. The second youngest in a farm family of nine, George had felt called to ministry with Canada's natives from an early age. During his Bible school years he did student ministry on neighboring reserves.

The denomination he chose to work with, the Christian and Missionary Alliance, advised him that if he were to work with natives in northern Canada, he should learn Cree. So he went to Meadow Lake, where Northern Canada Evangelical Mission offered instruction in the language.

When Bessie first saw George in church that fall, she wondered if the dark-haired young man might have some native background. And something told her that he might be her husband some day. But the thought left as quickly as it had come.

George, meanwhile, had also noticed Bessie. The mission

published a small magazine called *Northern Lights*, which relied on volunteers to fold, staple and put it in envelopes ready for mailing. Bessie had offered to help serve lunch to the volunteers one night when George was there, and the two were briefly introduced. Since she didn't look like a typical native girl, he wondered if maybe she was from the Middle East. The two didn't exchange much more than an introductory hello until a Halloween party at the church. Bessie and her roommate both went dressed as Bo Peep. George, true to his calling, arrived as an Indian chief. Although they didn't talk much during the party, at the end of the evening George asked the two Bo Peeps if he could walk them home.

"Sure," they answered together. Each one teased the other that it was she he was interested in. "He wants to walk you home," Bessie said to her roommate. "No, he's walking *you*," came the reply.

It wasn't long before George made it clear who he was interested in. He started asking Bessie out. George had a car, but because he didn't have enough money to run it, he and Bessie would walk to the corner café for hot chocolate, or review his Cree lessons together.

Having a personal tutor was a mixed blessing. George's classmates could tell when he had been studying with Bessie, because her Ojibway-influenced Cree was "corrupting" his language. His classmates began teasing him when he made mistakes. "We know where you were last night," they would tell him.

Although George and Bessie were interested in each other, neither was sure whether this was meant to be a long-term relationship. They broke off the relationship around Christmas, but remained on friendly terms.

The following summer Bessie and her friend Elvera went on a summer missions trip to the Interlake area of Manitoba. There they led vacation Bible schools and summer camps, traveling to different communities for a week at a time. Bessie enjoyed the work, but she wasn't convinced it was something she wanted to do as a single person.

Besides, she still had some exploring to do.

✖✚✖✚✖

With only a vague plan, Bessie got on a train in Manitoba and headed back east to Sioux Lookout, Ontario. It had been nine years since she had left northern Ontario with her parents.

Arriving in Sioux Lookout at about 3 a.m., she asked a taxi driver to take her to her former landlady's home, not even knowing if she still lived there. Mr. Weisenberg had since died, and she hadn't had contact with Mrs. Weisenberg for a long time. And even if she was still there, how would she react? Would she accept her former boarder after all these years?

"Are they expecting you?" the driver asked the young woman as he carried her luggage up the walk.

"I think so," Bessie replied with as much confidence as she could muster.

"Just set the bags here," she added, motioning to the front step, "and I'll be okay."

With relief she discovered the porch door was unlatched, so she could go in. Then she rang the doorbell. The house was completely dark.

A few minutes later Mrs. Weisenberg peered through the window. Who could possibly be ringing her doorbell at this hour of the night? When she saw a young woman standing at the door, she opened it.

"It's me—Bessie." Nine years had turned a teenager into a young woman, and it took a moment for Mrs. Weisenberg to recognize the person standing before her.

"Bessie!" Her former landlady was so happy to see her. The two talked until six in the morning, catching up on the years. Quite a switch from the twelve-year-old who didn't talk at all that first year in school.

Bessie did have an idea of what she wanted to do. She had applied to the Indian hospital in Sioux Lookout but hadn't heard back. So the next day she went to see the matron, who was friendly and interested in getting help from someone who already had hospital experience and who also knew the language the patients spoke.

Before long she had a job, and moved into the nurses' residence near the hospital.

Some of the patients came in from the north, where Bessie had grown up. Sometimes they remembered Bessie and her family, and reminisced with her about life at Big Trout Lake. It was one of those patients who informed Bessie that long before her mother had married her father, she had been married to someone else. Even though Bessie was now a young adult, her mother had never told her about the sorrow of her past. Later, when Bessie asked her father about it, he said Christina only got upset if someone mentioned the past. So Bessie never talked to her mother about it.

※◇※✦◇◇✦※◇※

She wasn't there long before she received a letter. It was from George McPeek, and it was postmarked Loon Lake, Alberta, but had travelled to Meadow Lake, Saskatchewan, to be forwarded to Hodgson, Manitoba, where Bessie had spent the summer, before it finally reached its recipient in Sioux Lookout, Ontario.

George had been thinking. He enjoyed the mission work, but wouldn't it be better to have a partner? He remembered the young woman he had begun to get acquainted with in Meadow Lake, and wondered if she would be interested in resuming a relationship.

The two corresponded for several months, and George suggested Bessie move out to Alberta, where he was quite certain she could get a job at the Peace River hospital. He knew the matron there, as he often brought patients into the hospital from the more isolated communities.

So in July 1964 Bessie moved again. She got a job at the hospital, and although George lived in another community, the two were able to see each other often enough to become reacquainted. Before long they both felt like they were meant for each other and were engaged in the fall.

It was Christmas morning, 1964. Bessie woke up with a swollen, painful throat. She had the mumps!

She was staying at George's sister's house in Edmonton. Just the night before, George had presented her with an engagement ring. The two were to be married on January 16 in Meadow Lake, in the church where they had met. She had just quit her hospital job, and the Christmas holidays were to be spent shopping for a wedding dress and getting ready for the wedding.

And here she was, sick in bed. The temperature was minus 40, far too cold to venture outside, and unwise for someone who had contracted a contagious disease. Bessie was helpless.

But Ruth, her soon-to-be sister-in-law, quickly swung into action, shopping for patterns and fabric samples and bringing them back to the ailing Bessie, who chose the dress style she wanted. Ruth deftly made the wedding dress, and Bessie and George were able to keep their wedding date.

Despite the cold spell, January 16, 1965 was an unbelievably warm day in Meadow Lake. Snow was melting and water was dripping off the roofs. Bessie's sister Esther and George's sister Linda were bridesmaids, while Bessie's brother Herb and

126   *Keepers of the Faith*

Helmet, a friend of George's, served as groomsmen. The only unfortunate aspect to the day was that Bessie's parents, who had been serving as relief missionaries, were snowbound in northern Manitoba and couldn't make it out to the wedding.

⚜⚜⚜

The early months of their marriage were spent in Luseland, Saskatchewan, where George was an interim pastor. Then the couple went about raising their support for a missionary assignment in Churchill, Manitoba.

They arrived in Churchill, on the western shore of the Hudson Bay, in August. As Manitoba's most northern town, Churchill was a mixture of Inuit, Dene and Cree Indians, and whites, all of whom lived in separate settlements. It was George and Bessie's job to work with the Crees, who lived in rough shacks along the river flats. Many of them weren't treaty Indians, so they didn't get help from the government. Most were extremely poor.

George and Bessie lived in the town of Churchill, but rented a small building on the flats where they held Cree services. Bessie helped with women's Bible studies and sewing circles, as well as children's clubs. This was the role she wanted, working together with her partner.

It wasn't long, however, before she took on another role. Soon after she was married, Bessie became pregnant. The joy of anticipating a new life soon gave way to sorrow when she miscarried after five months.

The doctor examined her and did several tests. There appeared to be something wrong.

"You'll never be able to carry a pregnancy to term," he concluded.

Was he right? Was it true that she would never give birth to a lively, healthy baby?

Bessie longed to have children, so she prayed. God, she knew, was able to do more than any earthly doctor. If God wanted her to have children, He would see to it that she would be able to.

Again she remembered Psalm 139, how God had known her while she was still in her mother's womb. If God had made her, He could also form a tiny child within her and watch over it until birth.

Shortly after her miscarriage, Bessie got pregnant again and was sick for a long time. She spent months in bed, worried about losing this baby, too. But in August 1966, she gave birth to her first son, Kenton, who weighed almost eight pounds. He was healthy and thriving! She thanked God for changing the impossible into the possible.

❖❖❖❖❖❖❖❖

George was thinking about a change. For a long time he had been interested in teaching, and wondered if it was time for him to go back to school. So the young family packed up after two years in Churchill and moved to Thunder Bay, Ontario, where he entered teachers' college. The couple's second son, Jordan, was born there in December 1967.

George and Bessie also became house parents to fifteen native boys who were in Thunder Bay to attend school. Bessie's parents came to help them out. A house full of busy and sometimes rebellious Grade 9 boys was a challenge. Bessie and her mother had to cook, clean, and do laundry for fifteen teenagers. After Bessie gave birth to Jordan, just after Christmas, another woman came to help one day a week.

George finished his teachers' training after a year, and the family moved to Weagamow, an isolated community not far from where Bessie had grown up. He taught there for one year before they moved back to Churchill, where he got a job at the elementary school. It was there that the McPeeks' third son, Dana, was born in October 1970.

Life was never dull. The couple took in foster children, sometimes two or three at a time. At one point they were caring for two little sisters and considering adoption. Then the grandmother decided she would take them. Bessie had become attached to the little girls, and it was heart-breaking to let them go. After that she decided she couldn't take in any more children if she would only have to say goodbye to them later.

After two years in Churchill they moved a couple hundred miles south to the town of Gillam, where they stayed three years. During the summers they went south to Winnipeg, so George could further his education at the University of Manitoba.

Their time in Gillam got off to a rough start when they arrived and the teacher's residence wasn't ready; the family had to go to a hotel. When they finally got into their house, it hadn't been cleaned properly. Not only that, but Bessie was very sick.

Thankfully, a kind neighbor took over the cleaning and preparation of the residence. Even though she didn't know the family that had just moved to town, she willingly unpacked boxes, cleaned up the kitchen and babysat.

Bessie was grateful for the help. She was in horrible pain with a high fever. She had begun feeling sick when they left Winnipeg, but now it was worse. She ended up in the hospital.

She was diagnosed with a kidney infection and was flown out a couple of times to Winnipeg over the next months for medical treatment.

Then one day John Goodrich, a missionary pilot, came to visit. "Can I pray for you?" he asked Bessie.

She willingly agreed. He anointed her with oil and asked God to heal her. And He did. From that day on Bessie didn't have to take any more medicine, and she wasn't bothered any more by kidney infection. Truly God had healed her affliction, just as He had allowed her to carry not one but three babies to term, against medical predictions.

<hr/>

After several years in the teaching profession, George was expanding his horizons again. He had long been interested in literature ministry, and an opportunity was opening up in Cass Lake, Minnesota, where there was a Bible school for native students and a literature department.

The Christian and Missionary Alliance printed a small paper called *The Indian Christian*. George took over as editor and publisher, and under his leadership, the paper flourished. Circulation grew from 850 to about 7,000. Obviously there was a need for literature to reach native North Americans.

The McPeeks stayed in Cass Lake from 1974 to 1977. George wanted to continue the work, but he felt he needed more training. So the next move was to Wheaton, Illinois, where he enrolled in a master's program in journalism and communications.

He took the literature ministry with him, publishing from the basement of the family home. The two years there were busy, as he was a full-time student and a full-time editor and publisher. Several people helped out during those years, including Hulda Baltzer and George's niece, Cheryl O'Neill. But the work didn't pay very much, so Bessie took in a couple of boarders and worked part-time in the college cafeteria to help make ends meet.

The future looked great. George was excited about all the new things he was learning, and looking forward to putting them into practice once he graduated and got back to devoting all his energies to publishing. *The Indian Christian* was planning a merger with another publication, *Indian Life*, whose South Dakota-based publisher was wanting to retire and hoped George would take it over.

Then, just before he was to graduate, his boss came to visit. George was eager to tell him about all the plans he had for the literature ministry.

"I have something to tell you," the boss said soberly. It seemed the denomination was planning to make some changes. More money and effort would be put into church-planting, and less into support ministries such as literature.

"We're planning to close down the publication," he continued.

George and Bessie were stunned by the blow. How could things look so promising in one moment, only to be flattened the next?

What should they do now?

⬥⬥⬥⬥⬥

If there really was a need for literature ministry to natives, and George believed there was, there had to be a way of sustaining it. George contacted some of the missions distributing the paper and asked them what they thought.

Most didn't want to see the paper stop publishing. So after graduation from Wheaton, George gathered together a handful of mission leaders from the United States and Canada and formed a new organization, Intertribal Christian Communications (Intercom), which would publish *Indian Life*.

The board decided Winnipeg, Manitoba would be a good central location for the new ministry. For the McPeeks, it meant a return to Canada.

It was 1979 and they had moved a lot during their fourteen years of marriage. The children had always adapted to their new surroundings, making friends easily wherever they went. Now in Grades 3, 7 and 8, the McPeek boys made it known they were ready to stay in one place for a while.

"We're not moving anymore," they announced to their parents when they arrived in Winnipeg.

Whether their words were a threat or a prophecy, they came true. The McPeeks stayed in Winnipeg for the next sixteen years.

God provided the family with a large house at a reasonable price, and with it the option to buy a business selling beads and leather. For Bessie, it was an answer to prayer. Taking over a business was a way of supplementing the family income while fledgling Intercom was getting off the ground.

It also brought Bessie back to her roots and provided her with a ministry of her own. At first, Bessie's Indian Craft Supplies was primarily a mail order business, started in the basement of the house. Though the only advertising was the occasional flyer sent to nearby reserves, bead-workers from far and wide began ordering their supplies from Bessie.

Over time, she felt she got to know many of her customers, who appreciated being able to talk to their supplier in their own language. Not only that, but they found in Bessie a sympathetic listener. Sometimes they would pour their hearts out over the phone, telling her about their struggles and asking her to pray for them.

It didn't hurt that when Bessie sent out their orders, she

always included a copy of *Indian Life* or some other literature with the package. Her clients came to look forward to this bonus, and if ever an order arrived without something to read, they would ask about it. Even though the business had her name on it, she always considered it to be God's business, and He honored that attitude by blessing it.

Eventually some of her customers wanted to see where they got their supplies from, and when they came to town they visited Bessie. The McPeeks later moved the business to a corner store, where walk-in traffic made it grow even more. By that time the three boys were adults, and helped out in the business.

<hr />

For many years Leslie and Christina Garrett moved about the north, spending a few months here and a few years there helping out where needed. By 1979, when Bessie and George moved to Winnipeg, they were getting older and were ready to slow down—at least a little.

They too moved to Winnipeg, where they lived with the McPeek family and continued to minister to those they came in contact with. They enjoyed meeting with customers who came from all over the north to Bessie's bead shop. And every Tuesday they went to a large nearby hospital, where they visited native patients, especially those from out of town.

They continued that ministry for ten years, blessing many lonely and frightened people who were more than grateful to speak to someone who understood their language and their ways when they came to the city for medical care.

In the fall of 1989, the McPeek sons planned a surprise party in honor of their parents' twenty-fifth anniversary. Although the anniversary didn't officially happen until January, October seemed like the best time to have the party.

Two months later, on December 18, Leslie Garrett had a heart attack. He was taken to the hospital, where he died two days later. He was ninety-one. He had devoted many years to serving the Ojibway and Cree peoples of northern Canada. He had endured hardships and heartaches. He had been a faithful servant. It was time for him to see his God face to face and to hear His words, "Well done."

✦✦✦✦✦✦

Christina Garrett was lonely. She had lost her life's partner, and her daughter and grandsons were away from home during the day working at the shop. The days were too empty.

When an apartment opened up at a nearby seniors' home for natives, Christina moved in. There she found friends who could speak her language. She stayed there for a year.

In the summer of 1995, Christina was about to celebrate her eighty-fifth birthday. Her younger daughter and her husband came for a visit that summer, as well as old friends from Big Trout Lake. A week before her birthday, Bessie organized a party so the out-of-town people could celebrate with her.

The following Friday night she said she wasn't feeling well. Bessie called the doctor, who came down to look at her. She seemed fine, but just to be sure, he suggested she go in for some tests on her heart after the weekend.

On Sunday, July 3, the day of her birthday, Bessie went to the seniors' home with a big cake to share with Christina's new friends, and with people who came from the church to say hello. It was a special time. Everyone greeted her and hugged her. She was very much loved.

Bessie talked to her mother on the phone several times that evening, but when she phoned the next day, there was no answer. Thinking Christina was out visiting her friends in the lounge, Bessie tried again later.

Still no answer. Bessie began to worry. She quickly went down to the seniors' home and entered her mother's apartment.

Christina Garrett had joined her husband in heaven. She had happily celebrated her birthday, and after everyone left, she, too, had died of a heart attack. It had happened quickly and she had not suffered.

✦✦✦✦✦✦✦

That summer was a blur. Two of Bessie's sons, Jordan and Dana, got married within six weeks of each other. Her mother had died in between, and now, at the end of August, she and George were moving again.

After sixteen years of working hard to build the ministry of

Indian Life, which had expanded beyond a magazine to a book-publishing business, it was time for a change. The magazine itself has reached a circulation of 60,000 all over North America.

The last few years had been especially busy. After George resigned from Intercom in the fall of 1992, he was associate pastor at First Nations Community Church. At the same time, he and Bessie had been travelling throughout North America with Art and Betty Holmes, giving Grieving Indian seminars, based on a book by the same name.

Published in 1988 and co-written by Art and George, *The Grieving Indian* was a way of reaching natives who suffered from the fallout of drug and alcohol abuse, as well as the emotional losses that came from cultural changes, especially the grief of broken families when children were sent to residential schools.

The book quickly became popular, with Indian bands inviting George and Art to conduct healing seminars on reserves and in towns and cities. Although the book was based on Christian principles, many natives, Christian and non-Christian, were eager to learn from it.

While George organized the seminars and Art did the teaching, Bessie and Arthur's wife Betty helped with book sales. Both couples were involved in counseling, but the women especially liked to talk to Bessie and Betty.

Unexpectedly, Bessie herself found healing at one of the seminars for a wound she hadn't realized she carried. A woman approached her after a seminar wanting to talk. She had had a miscarriage and was grieving over it. Her grief made Bessie realize that after she had miscarried her first pregnancy in 1965, she had immediately gone on with life without allowing herself to mourn her loss. Meeting this woman made her remember, and the two were able to help each other.

By the spring of 1994 George felt the Lord was leading him to another venture. But he didn't know what. The one thing he sensed was that the Lord would let him know some time in January 1995.

The McPeeks celebrated their thirtieth anniversary on January 16, 1995. They still didn't know what they would be doing next. While Bessie tended to be anxious, George was confident God would let them know in the right time. Bessie took comfort in one of her favorite promises, Deuteronomy 31:8: "It is the Lord who goes before you; He will be with you, He will not fail you or forsake you; do not fear or be dismayed." It was a promise that had sustained her many times over many changes, ever since she was a young girl.

On the evening of January 31, George and Bessie came home to find a message on their answering machine. Neil Foster, head of The Christian and Missionary Alliance publishing house, wanted to talk to George.

"Would you consider becoming editorial director of Christian Publishers?" he asked George when the two connected.

The invitation had come in the last few hours of January. The Lord had kept His promise to George.

✖✧✖✦✧✖✦✖✧✖

After thinking and praying about it, and going for an interview, George and Bessie decided it was the right move to make. Their sons were all grown and could stay behind to carry on their own work and family life.

In August 1995, the McPeeks moved from Winnipeg to Pennsylvania, where the publishing house was located. They found a place to live in Mechanicsburg, not far from the publishing company in Camp Hill.

While George settled into his work heading the editorial department, Bessie found a job in purchasing, where her previous experience in mail order business came in handy. Their youngest son, Dana, and his wife bought the craft supply business.

In the spring of 2001 the McPeeks moved again, this time back to Minnesota where George had first become involved in publishing. This time his main focus would not be on publishing, however, but on church planting, pastoring a small native church.

George McPeek, the farm boy from southern Saskatchewan, has spent most of his adult years working and living with native people, like his father-in-law before him. He had always felt comfortable with Native Americans, and called to minister to them.

Bessie McPeek has moved many times in her life. Each time, she has had to claim the promise of God that He would go before her. Each time, that promise has sustained her in facing the unknown. She knows for a certainty the words from Deuteronomy 31:8: "It is the Lord who goes before you; He will be with you, He will not fail you or forsake you; do not fear or be dismayed."

Only the Lord knows if there will be more moves ahead for the McPeeks. "The Lord has shown before that He will never forsake us," Bessie says. "So we can face the future with confidence, and without fear, knowing that God is our leader."

LIZZIE YORK

Looking for Love

Canada's Arctic can seem cold and desolate to people who make their home in the South, but to those whose way of life is rooted in the tundra and snow, it's warm, familiar and secure.

On May 28, 1954, Lizzie Epoo was born into an Inuit family on Patterson Island. It was nearing summer, and since the family was nomadic, Lizzie was born in a tent. She was the second daughter born to Lazarusie and Amilia (Emily) Epoo, but since another family had adopted her older sister, she was the eldest to grow up in the Epoo household. Three brothers and a sister followed.

When Lizzie was only six months old, her mother became sick with tuberculosis, and had to go south for medical care. She spent years in the hospital, both in Hamilton, Ontario, and in Moose Factory. Both places were thousands of miles away from home, too far to visit, so Lizzie's grandmother Anna became the maternal figure in her life. Anna's home would often be filled with friends praying and studying the Bible in Inuktitut.

Lizzie formed a close bond with Grandmother Anna, who was a very gentle, loving woman. Whenever Lizzie saw Anna, she would run and give her grandmother a big hug. Her grandmother made her feel very secure.

Anna was a very godly woman. She loved to read from the Bible and study it, and taught Lizzie the importance of prayer. When Lizzie was still a young child, Anna went blind. She contracted glaucoma and lost her eyesight very quickly. There was no easy access to medical treatment then, the way there is now. When a person in a northern community needs urgent medical attention, a plane is sent in to take the person to a clinic or hospital.

Still Anna prayed, asking God to allow her to see her grandchildren once in a while.

And God granted her that request. Sometimes in the early mornings, Lizzie recalls, her grandmother would be able to see the children sleeping—one granddaughter in the bed beside her, and Lizzie and her brother at her feet. She would watch them and admire them for several minutes before losing her sight again.

In those days, Arctic children had no notion of manufactured toys or games. They played outside in the snow and on the rocks, using their imagination to transform rocks into dolls. Nature was a friend: kids would jump on the huge pieces of ice floating on the sea in summer, or play tag on the tundra or snow.

In the winter the family would build an igloo, keeping it cosy with a fire and heating it with an oil lamp. It was a comfortable place to live.

Lizzie's father did the family hunting and fishing, fetching seal, bearded seal, caribou, and varieties of fish, like cod, char, and trout. Lizzie's favorite food was caribou, but she liked other kinds of meat, too, cooked, raw or frozen.

When Lizzie was old enough to go to school, the Epoo family shed the nomadic lifestyle and moved into a house in a community. Lizzie wasn't too happy about that. The house was so dry, and at first she couldn't sleep. There seemed to be no air, unlike the igloo she was used to, which had just the right humidity.

School also changed Lizzie's life. She had to speak English, and learn certain manners which seemed foreign to her. In Inuit culture, for example, people don't use any word for "please" because it sounds too much like begging. Instead, they would gesture, or use a particular tone of voice to indicate they wanted something.

The school seemed strict, and too full of rules. Nevertheless,

Lizzie liked to learn, and even when she came home from school her father would teach her reading and spelling in both the Roman alphabet used in English and the syllabics used for Inuktitut.

Lizzie's parents didn't want her to go away to school, and because there was no advanced schooling in their community, she quit after Grade six, when she was thirteen years old. She quickly got a job at the same school as an interpreter for the kindergarten children, as well as a teaching assistant. Later she went to the Hudson's Bay Company, the main—and usually, the only—retail store in the North, where she worked as a clerk.

No matter what kind of job she had, Lizzie made sure she had time to read and study. She loved learning.

✷✷✷✦✷✷✦✷✷

Early one morning when Lizzie was thirteen her mother woke her up to tell her the sad news: her grandmother had died during the night of heart failure. Lizzie was heartbroken. She loved her grandmother so much, more than anyone in the world.

"Can I see her?" Lizzie asked. "Can I say goodbye?"

The answer was no. The women of the community were already washing Grandmother Anna and preparing her for burial. They wouldn't let the young girl say her last goodbye.

Lizzie was angry and hurt. And she made a decision: "I decided never to love anyone again because it hurt too much."

Lizzie was sixteen years old when she learned the hard way about how life starts. She had a boyfriend, and figured when they had sex it was just some sort of game. She thought babies were found in the storm, or came down the chimney or were delivered from heaven. No one talked about how they were born or how they were conceived. It wasn't until she was pregnant herself that she found out.

She stayed home for six months before her parents sent her south to Montreal, Quebec, to have her baby. Montreal was a big city, and an exciting one. There was so much to see and do. So many people to meet. It was a completely new world for her.

While she was waiting to give birth to her baby, she volunteered to interpret for other Inuit people who found themselves in the strange city with no English language skills to help them. Fluent in both English and Inuktitut, and adept at interpreting, Lizzie visited numerous other hospitals to help.

Her parents had told her right from the start that she was too young to raise a child. They announced that they would raise the baby daughter, born in 1970, a common practice among Inuit. Lizzie went along with her parents' idea, although she stayed at home till her daughter was five.

She worked at various jobs, interpreting at the local nursing station, teaching school and working at a radio station, where she was an announcer, operated the console and prepared news items. There she stayed for about three years, enjoying the variety and responsibility.

Lizzie's family had always been church-going people. The Anglican church had long been established throughout the Arctic, and virtually everyone attended services on Sundays. Lizzie went automatically, because it was just something people did. But church was strict. She had to sit very still and stiff, and couldn't play or fidget. Even though the services were in Inuktitut, they held limited meaning for her.

By the time she was sixteen, her church attendance dropped off. She didn't feel like she was good enough to go to church. But then she felt guilty for not going, because she was taught that she was supposed to go every Sunday.

As an older teen and a young woman, she began traveling and experiencing more, and that's when she found out that church didn't have to be dull and boring. There was action in church, and that wasn't bad at all.

She started going more regularly again, and reading the Bible a lot, but there was still something that wasn't quite right. Even when she read the Bible, she didn't understand what she was reading.

<hr />

In 1977, when Lizzie was twenty-three, she left her parents' home and moved to Kujjuaq, a town of about two thousand people on the Ungava Coast in the far north of Quebec. There she started seeing a young man named Alan York, whom she had met in

Toronto a couple of years earlier. It was at a Canadian heritage show, where people from different regions of the country demonstrated cultural skills and practices. Lizzie went along as an interpreter with an Inuit group of kayak builders.

Although Alan was from the south, he had been living in Kujjuaq. He was back in Toronto to study plumbing and heating, and decided to take in the cultural program.

Lizzie didn't like him at first. Even when she moved to Kujjuaq and met him again, she still didn't like him. But she kept coming into contact with him because he was a friend of her current boyfriend. When she and the boyfriend broke up, she and Alan became friends. They were married in 1979.

❧❧❧❧❧❧❧

One morning in 1988, Lizzie was at home alone. Her husband had gone to work and her children—Jusi, Patricia and Bryan—had gone to school. She was feeling a lot of pain in her hands from the eczema that had bothered her for years. The pain had been so bad that at one stage she wasn't able to work for four years.

She was also feeling sorry for herself. As had happened so many times before, she had blood poisoning from the eczema and had had to soak her hands in a special solution that morning.

She didn't normally cry when things bothered her. When her grandmother Anna died in 1968 she had closed herself to showing emotional pain, determined she would never love anyone the way she loved her grandmother, because she didn't want to suffer the pain of losing someone else.

But that morning Lizzie began to weep. She looked at her hands, and suddenly she thought of a pain that was far worse than the physical pain of her eczema. She began to think about the "pit of fire" that she had learned about as a little girl. She worried that if her soul wasn't prepared, she would go to that pit when she died. She didn't think she was a nice enough person to go to heaven to live with God instead.

Lizzie cried long and loud. She needed to cry out all the emotional and spiritual pain that had built up in her. Suddenly, she started to see things differently.

In front of her was a small shape, and within seconds the shape turned into a little girl about eleven or twelve years old. The little girl was dirty, with black marks all over her skin and clothes.

"Who is this person?" Lizzie wondered. Then she recognized the girl: it was herself. It was her soul, which had never matured beyond the time she was thirteen, when her grandmother died and she cut herself off from feeling.

The little girl in the vision was afraid of her. She hurt every time Lizzie said or did something that hurt someone else. Looking at her, Lizzie couldn't help but love her. She felt sorry for the little girl and didn't want to do anything more to hurt her.

"I had so much love for that soul," Lizzie recalls. "I wanted to understand what love was, because I had forgotten."

In a matter of seconds she began understanding. God spoke to her.

"I have listened to your prayers," he told her, "but I have not answered them yet because nobody comes to My kingdom except through My Son."

At that moment, Lizzie realized she wanted to enter the kingdom of heaven. She knelt down on the floor, repented of her sins and gave her life to Christ.

⬥⬥⬥⬥⬥⬥

After that experience, Lizzie's life changed. Now when she read the Bible she understood what it was saying. She had so much hunger for God's Word for the next three or four years. She couldn't seem to get enough of it.

About three weeks after her conversion, Lizzie read a book about healing. She read that people can be physically healed from diseases. She wanted healing from her eczema. She wanted a new piece of skin.

It took a lot of courage, but finally Lizzie went to talk to a woman in the community who had offered to pray for healing if she ever wanted it. Lizzie was a little nervous about going to her: she had thought healing only happened in the time of Jesus.

Nevertheless, she went for prayer, and within a week her eczema disappeared. Her hands and her feet were healed from the painful disease! It never returned after that.

⬥⬥⬥⬥⬥⬥

Lizzie's new, vibrant faith changed her in other ways, too. She used to be very stubborn, for one thing. She was very blunt and direct, and if she didn't have time for someone, she let them know. But after she committed her life to Jesus in 1988 she began to mellow.

At first her husband thought she was too preoccupied with her faith. But Lizzie was determined that nothing in her life would ever be more important than her faith in Christ. When she came home from a conference one time, she informed him: "Whatever God wills, I do." Everything else came second. Even if it meant losing her husband, she would not compromise.

At first Alan didn't answer. But two days later, realizing his wife was serious about her faith, he told her: "I will back you up." A few years later he, too, accepted Jesus into his life.

Lizzie was having strange dreams and visions. They always meant something, but understanding what was sometimes difficult. One dream was about a church. It was in a whirlwind. It came to Lizzie that where the Spirit of the Lord is, nothing can be withheld. The Spirit comes like a great, rushing wind and moves where it wills.

Another dream was about her mother. Lizzie saw that she had fish in her cupboards.

"Mom," she asked in her dream, "what are you doing with fish in the cupboards?"

When she woke up she understood: her mother was passing the work that she had not completed on to her daughter. That work was fishing for people, bringing them to Jesus.

In a third dream she felt as if her soul left her bed while she slept one night and moved to another house in the community. There she prayed with the family, which was troubled by evil spirits. She named a spirit, and a huge snake appeared. She prayed, holding the snake in her left hand. An earlier prophecy had shown her that God wanted to use her left hand, and this vision confirmed it. The experience was so powerful that her whole body moved as she slept, waking up her husband. Then the vision ended.

On another occasion Lizzie spent a week teaching and sharing with two sisters who were seeking God. The time was very intense as the three were constantly battling evil spirits in the village. The sisters felt much fear, but at the same time they longed for God to speak to them. Lizzie discerned that neither of the young women had ever accepted Christ, so they were not protected from fear of evil. That week Lizzie led both of them into a relationship with Jesus.

The morning after the younger sister came to the Lord, Lizzie heard the spirit of Jesus speak through her. Her whole body shook as she praised God, because she was hearing the voice of God.

"Because you have a humble heart," God told the young woman, "I have chosen you to be the captain of the spiritual warriors." God was setting her apart for special ministry.

Even though she had a responsible job, a growing family and an active ministry, there was still something missing in Lizzie's life. She knew what it was, too: it was love. Since her grandmother's death, she had never really felt she understood what love was. And she had not allowed herself to really love, either, because she didn't want to get hurt again if she lost someone close to her.

"What is love?" she would ask people she respected. They never gave her any satisfactory answers. "You are love," one person told her. That just confused her more. Finally she quit asking.

At that time she was executive director of the Nunavik Regional Board of Health and Social Services, overseeing health and social services throughout the fourteen communities of northern Quebec. In that capacity she went to Reykjavik, Iceland, for an international health conference. After the conference, the Icelandic hosts arranged for a tour to a famous hot spring in the country's interior.

As she watched the water steam and roil and finally work itself up and shoot high into the air, Lizzie was reminded of a woman in labor.

"How awesome God is!" Lizzie thought. "How wondrous are His works!" The exploding stream of water was like love to her. She felt it, for the first time, throughout her whole being. Suddenly it felt like she, too, would explode. She screamed: once, and again.

Then she felt better. Finally, she felt she understood what love was: an overwhelming, overpowering shower from God.

※◆※◆※◆※

In 1992 Lizzie attended a conference on healing in Edmonton, Alberta. Many Inuit people who had been hurt in the past, from forced moves or settlement, from abuse or other wounds, were starting to find spiritual and emotional healing.

There were three thousand people at the conference. On the last day a Native man was telling the people there about grieving.

"Close your eyes," he said. Lizzie closed her eyes.

"Think about the person that you loved most in your life." Immediately Lizzie thought of her grandmother, Anna.

She was a little girl again, only four or five years old. She saw her grandmother so vividly, and in her mind she ran up to her and threw her arms around her in a big hug. She felt that same security she had felt as a child. She was enjoying that moment so much.

Then the speaker said something else. "Let her go. She is dead. Accept her death."

The pain hit Lizzie. She exploded in tears of grief over her grandmother's death. They were tears she had never cried before. She had never allowed herself to properly grieve Anna's death.

It wasn't over instantly. Lizzie grieved for several years after that, but it was good. It helped her to become more mellow and accepting.

Over the years Lizzie worked her way through the regional government system in a series of jobs. Because the regional government was newly formed when she started, there was a lot of work to do, including negotiating with the Quebec provincial government. She went from translating to management, and worked at funding, development and creating new jobs. She left work for a while when she was pregnant, but returned later.

In 1984 she was appointed executive director of health and social services for the region. She worked at the position until 1999, when the board chair called her into his office.

"I've got bad news," he told her. "You're fired."

"Why?" she asked him, stunned.

"You're not a team leader. You dictate too much. You're absent too much. You have worked here too long. You haven't succeeded in making the financial transition and you should concentrate on your religious life. We don't need your services anymore."

Lizzie was hurt. The things he was saying to her were not true. And she had never let her personal life or her faith interfere with her work. "I never did anything that would make me feel guilty," she says.

She lodged a complaint with the human rights department, but decided, at the same time, not to let the wrongful dismissal hold her back. She still had volunteer work to do in the church and community, she still had part-time or contract work, and she had a newly adopted daughter to look after.

As a member of the Anglican church, Lizzie has been involved in every level of church life, from the local parish and the Diocese of the Arctic to the national governing body, called the Council of General Synod.

God is moving in the Arctic church, and Lizzie believes the spiritual vitality there needs to be brought to the South. When she attends church meetings in southern Canada, it seems people are so concerned about following the agenda that they don't allow the Holy Spirit to lead them. "It saddens me to see that," she says.

But Lizzie is not afraid to speak out at national meetings on controversial issues like homosexuality. She firmly believes in sticking with what the Bible says. And the Bible is the Word of God.

"It's my God that I want to please more than anything else."

Do you know the Creator's Son?

After reading *Keepers of the Faith*, do you feel that Jesus truly is the Creator God's Son? Is He speaking to you? Would you like to respond to what you have just read?

Here are five things you need to know to believe in Jesus as your Savior.

You need to:

REPENT—Be sorry for the wrong things you have done—sorry enough to quit doing them. "God did not remember these times when people did not know better. But now He tells all men everywhere to be sorry for their sins and to turn from them" Acts 17:30.

CONFESS—Tell God you have sinned. "If you say with your mouth that Jesus is Lord, and believe in your heart that God raised Him from the dead, you will be saved from the punishment of sin" Romans 10:9.

BELIEVE—Jesus died for you. "Put your trust in the Lord Jesus Christ and you...will be saved from the punishment of sin" Acts 16:31.

ASK—God to forgive you. "If we tell Him our sins, He is faithful and we can depend on Him to forgive us our sins. He will make our lives clean from all sin" 1 John 1:9.

RECEIVE—Jesus as your Savior. "He gave the right and the power to become children of God, to those who receive Him...to those who put their trust in His Name" John 1:12.

If you want to ask Jesus Christ into your life, pray the following prayer or pray in your own words:

Dear Jesus, I realize I am a sinner. I long for peace in my heart. I believe You are the Holy Son of God, that You came down and died on the cross for my sins. Thank You for doing this for me. I am sorry for my sins. Please forgive me.

With Your help, I will turn my back on them. By faith, I receive You into my life as my personal Savior and Lord. From now on, I want to please You. In Your name, Amen.

If you have followed these steps and asked Christ to take control of your life, get a copy of God's Word, the Bible, and begin reading it. Also start talking to God in prayer. Go to church regularly. Choose a church where God's message of salvation is taught.

If you have prayed the above prayer, the publishers of *Keepers of the Faith* would like to hear from you. Please write your name on the coupon below, or if you don't want to cut up this book just write on another sheet of paper and mail it to:

In Canada:
Indian Life Books, P.O. Box 3765, RPO Redwood Centre
Winnipeg MB R2W 3R6

In the U.S:
Indian Life Books, P.O. Box 32
Pembina ND 58271

I prayed the prayer suggested in *Keepers of the Faith* and now I would like more information on how to live as a Christian. Please write to me and tell me the name of someone who can give me personal help.

NAME _____

ADDRESS _____

TOWN/CITY _____

STATE/PROVINCE _____

ZIP/POSTAL _____

MORE GOOD READING FROM INDIAN LIFE BOOKS

GOD'S WARRIOR

This life story of Ray Prince, tells us about a World War II veteran and a veteran of many personal battles including residential school life, abuse and alcoholism. He found hope and healing in Jesus Christ and then committed himself to spreading the good news.

THE COUNCIL SPEAKS

A collection of answers to over 60 questions on life, tradition, culture and practical issues. These may have been questions you have had, but were afraid to ask. Join the circle and listen to the answers. They may change your life!

THE LONELY SEARCH

Albert Tait is an Oji-Cree man whose life God completely changed around. He went from being an unwanted orphan and an alcoholic, to a man of faith and a leader and teacher for Native believers. Discover how he found freedom from a curse and the source of all blessing.

THE CONQUERING INDIAN

An amazing collection of 70 stories showing that Jesus Christ can heal the deepest hurt of Native people. This book tells the stories of how these people, young and old, reached out to Jesus and how He answered their pleas and helped them to have victory over the problems they faced. You, too, can face up to your problems and conquer them. This book can be used to guide you to the One who can help you win that victory.

The Grieving Indian

Every Native person needs to read this book for the help and hope it offers. With over 70,000 books in print, find out why it has attracted so much attention.

Read one man's story of pain and hopelessness. Learn how his wife took a desperate step to turn his life around. This is a powerful book of hope and healing. Used by treatment centers and addictions counselors.

Whiteman's Gospel

"This is one book that should be read by every man and woman in North America," says Bill McCartney, founder of Promise Keepers. The author, Craig Stephen Smith, a Chippewa from the Leech Lake Reservation in northern Minnesota, examines Christianity and how it has affected Native North Americans. His experience led him to believe that change is desperately needed in both native and church communities.

Indian Life Newspaper

The most widely read Native publication in North America. In its pages you will find positive news of Indian people and events, first-person stories, photo features, family life articles, and much more. Published six times a year. Write for a free sample copy. Find out why over 100,000 people read this newspaper.

Video: Learning to Fly—The Path of Biblical Discipleship

A true-to-life story illustrates the challenges facing a new believer. This video will change your life and the life of your church by giving you a perspective on what discipleship is all about. It will show you why making disciples is so important. The Great Commission is more than making converts—it's making disciples. That's done through relationships.

Are you a first-time reader of Crying Wind's books?

Crying Wind wrote her first book entitled *Crying Wind,* as well as a second book, *My Searching Heart.* Both of these were bestsellers and have been translated into a number of languages.

Sequoyah Editions is pleased to present these two bestselling titles in a new combined volume. Once again you can thrill to the saga of Crying Wind as she writes frankly about past hurts and fears that resurfaced as she tried to begin a new life in Christ.

Stumbling upon Christ in her teen years, she found acceptance and encouragement through the patient, lovingkindness of a Christian couple. They encouraged her to move into life with Christ and into her gifting of poetic expression to share how past pain could not halt her walk with Jesus. The results are her artwork and three books!

Sequoyah Editions is also proud to present *When the Stars Danced—* Crying Wind's third book in the series. In this volume, she picks up where *My Searching Heart* left off. You'll laugh and cry with her as she shares the joys and sorrows of raising a family in two different cultures along with her experiences of loving people dearly and then having to let them go. This is perhaps Crying Wind's best book.

You can enjoy these books along with the thousands of others who have enjoyed reading her story.

Visit Crying Wind's website at www.cryingwind.com

You may order these books and more from Indian Life Books. Please write for a catalogue and price list. In the United States write: Indian Life Books, P.O. Box 32 Pembina, ND 58271.

In Canada write: Indian Life Books, P.O. Box 3765 RPO Redwood Centre, Winnipeg MB R2W 3R6.

Credit card orders may be placed by calling 1-800-665-9275 in the U.S. and Canada.